Pyramid of Behavior Interventions

Seven Keys to a Positive Learning Environment

Tom Hierck   Charlie Coleman   Chris Weber

Solution Tree | Press

a division of

Solution Tree

555 North Morton Street
Bloomington, IN 47404
800.733.6786 (toll free) / 812.336.7700
FAX: 812.336.7790

email: info@solution-tree.com
solution-tree.com

Visit **go.solution-tree.com/behavior** to download the reproducibles in this book.

Printed in the United States of America

15 14 13   3 4 5

Library of Congress Cataloging-in-Publication Data

Hierck, Tom.
  Pyramid of behavior interventions : seven keys to a positive learning environment / Tom Hierck, Charlie Coleman, Chris Weber.
     p. cm.
  Includes bibliographical references and index.
  ISBN 978-1-936765-06-5 (perfect bound) -- ISBN 978-1-936765-07-2 (library ed.) 1. Classroom environment. 2. Problem children--Behavior modification. 3. School improvement programs. I. Coleman, Charlie. II. Weber, Chris, Ed.D. III. Title.
  LB3013.H535 2011
  371.102'4--dc23
                                  2011020054

Solution Tree
Jeffrey C. Jones, CEO & President

Solution Tree Press
President: Douglas M. Rife
Publisher: Robert D. Clouse
Vice President of Production: Gretchen Knapp
Managing Production Editor: Caroline Wise
Senior Production Editor: Suzanne Kraszewski
Text Designer: Amy Shock
Cover Designer: Amy Shock

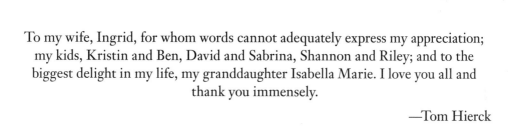

To my wife, Ingrid, for whom words cannot adequately express my appreciation; my kids, Kristin and Ben, David and Sabrina, Shannon and Riley; and to the biggest delight in my life, my granddaughter Isabella Marie. I love you all and thank you immensely.

—Tom Hierck

To my family—Deanie, Michael, and Ryan—for your patience and support.

—Charlie Coleman

To my mom and dad: you inspired me, and continue to inspire me, to do my best in service to society.

—Chris Weber

acknowledgments

Any success this book might have, any inspiration it might provide, can be traced to the many hands that helped to shape it. From the initial support of the Solution Tree team, and in particular Robb Clouse, Douglas Rife, Gretchen Knapp, and Claudia Wheatley, to the gentle nudges of the editorial team led by Suzanne Kraszewski, we appreciate their efforts to make a good thing better. Having a mentor like Wayne Hulley is a rare privilege, and his insights are evident throughout the text. Stubby McLean has been a tireless advocate, and his friendship has been truly appreciated. As the book evolved, friends like Nicole Vagle, Janet Malone, and Cassie Erkens provided helpful feedback. Colleagues that I'm fortunate to work with and others that I've met in my travels also offered fresh ideas. Thanks also to David Hierck, who put good advice ahead of Dad's feelings. Finally, thanks to old friend Charlie Coleman, who breathed life into a napkin years ago, and new friend Chris Weber, who shared comments that made me feel as if we've chatted forever.

—Tom Hierck

A project such as this requires the collaboration of so many. In addition to my own family, I would like to thank the entire team at Solution Tree for supporting me first as a staff developer and now as an author. Encouragement from the leaders of this top-notch organization, especially Jeff Jones and Robb Clouse, has helped me keep moving forward. Learning alongside such accomplished educators as Rick DuFour and Becky DuFour, as well as their cadre of PLC associates and authors, has pushed me to continually improve my own educational leadership, knowledge, and skills. A special thanks goes to Wayne Hulley, educator and entertainer, who wrote the foreward to this book. Detailed suggestions from "critical friends," particularly Suzanne Kraszewski and Dani Garner, have prompted me to refine my craft. Educators across North America, in schools where I have facilitated these concepts, have allowed me to share the collaborative skills required of all teacher-leaders who hope to improve the learning environment for all kids. The staff, students, and parents at the schools in British Columbia where I have been principal have pushed me to practice what I preach. Learning together, we have been able to put much of what is written in this book into daily practice. Your stories are the successes that bring this book to life.

A great deal of thanks goes to my coauthors, Tom and Chris. Chris Weber has added insight and polish to this work. Tom Hierck is not only a wise author and educator, but also a long-time friend who has helped take this idea from a napkin in an airport many years ago to the book that is in your hands today. It's been a long and entertaining road, my friend!

—Charlie Coleman

Our high expectations for students can only be achieved through collaborative practice, and the same was true during the completion of this book. Many people contributed to our efforts, starting with the great staff at Solution Tree, the foremost educational organization in North America. Thanks to Robb Clouse and the publishing team for their belief in this project and to Shannon Ritz and the professional development department for their support of our work.

Educators are the finest and most important professionals in our society. We have worked with amazing educators, particularly in Southern California and Chicago, and our thanks goes to them for the inspiration they provide us.

—Chris Weber

* * * * *

Solution Tree Press would like to thank the following reviewers:

Anne Cordasco
Assistant Principal
Andersen Junior High School
Chandler, Arizona

Jodi Frager
Counselor
Goodrich Middle School
Lincoln, Nebraska

Michael Fullan
Professor, Ontario Institute
for Studies in Education
University of Toronto
Toronto, Ontario

Karen Gaborik
Principal
Lathrop High School
Fairbanks, Alaska

Karen Harris
6th grade Social Studies Teacher
Arcadia Middle School
Rochester, New York

Laura S. McMahan
Principal
Lexington Middle School
Lexington, South Carolina

Sharon Miller
Principal
McKinley Middle School
Kenosha, Wisconsin

Melanie Monjure
Special Education Teacher
Old High Middle School
Bentonville, Arkansas

Kaye Otten
Behavior/Autism Specialist
Lee's Summit School District
Lee's Summit, Missouri

Jay Richard
Principal
Oyster River Middle School
Durham, New Hampshire

Angela Robinson
Principal
Sugarland Elementary School
Sterling, Virginia

Mary-Anne Smirle
Principal
Chilliwack Middle School
Chilliwack, British Columbia

Steve Spencer
Principal
LaCreole Middle School
Dallas, Oregon

Scott Tanner
Assistant Principal
Chula Vista High
Chula Vista, California

Linda Ward
Principal
St. Brigid Catholic School
Souffville, Ontario

Visit **go.solution-tree.com/behavior** to download the
reproducibles in this book.

table of contents

Tom Hierck, MA, an experienced educator since 1983, served as assistant superintendent of School District No. 46 (Sunshine Coast) in Gibsons, British Columbia, and principal in the Kootenay Lake School District in British Columbia. He also served with the Ministry of Education. Tom is a compelling presenter, infusing his message of hope with strategies culled from the real world.

Tom is a contributing author to *The Teacher as Assessment Leader* and *The Principal as Assessment Leader.* He has presented to schools and districts across North America with a message of celebration for educators seeking to make a difference in the lives of students. Tom's dynamic presentations explore the importance of positive learning environments and the role of assessment to improve student learning. His belief that "every student is a success story waiting to be told" has led him to work with teachers and administrators to create positive school cultures and build effective relationships that facilitate learning for all students.

Tom was a recipient of the Queen's Golden Jubilee Medallion, presented by the Premier and Lieutenant-Governor of British Columbia, for being a recognized leader in the field of public education.

Tom earned his master's degree at Gonzaga and his bachelor's degree and teacher certification at the University of British Columbia.

To learn more about Tom's work, visit www.tomhierck.com, follow him on Twitter @umakadiff, or visit his blog (http://umakeadiff.blogspot.com).

Charlie Coleman, MEd, is principal of Cowichan Secondary School in Duncan, British Columbia, where he is leading the staff to build a results-oriented professional learning community (PLC). He has been a principal at the elementary, middle, and secondary levels in ethnically and socioeconomically diverse communities. Charlie is former principal at Quamichan Middle School and Khowhemun Elementary School, and he has also been involved with the Ministry of Education School Improvement Project in a variety of middle and high school settings. He is a certified staff developer who combines his experience and expertise with an engaging sense of humor in his workshops and presentations.

As former principal of Khowhemun Elementary School, Charlie brought students and staff through challenges familiar to many socioeconomically disadvantaged communities. Four years after he became principal, the percentage of all Khowhemun students who met or exceeded expected scores in math and reading (based on the British Columbia Performance Standards) increased significantly. At Quamichan Middle School, Charlie's PLC team increased reading scores significantly (as measured by the District Reading Test) and significantly improved the transition rates for the vulnerable Aboriginal population.

Charlie's accomplishments earned him the Association for Supervision and Curriculum Development Outstanding Young Educator Award. He has also received Canada's Outstanding Principal Award from The Learning Partnership, and Khowhemun Elementary was named a Top 40 School in Canada by *Today's Parent Magazine*. He has published several articles in the United States and Canada and has served on numerous educational committees and teams.

A firm believer in servant leadership, Charlie uses his knowledge and energy to help other educators achieve great results. In addition, his experience working with urban and Native Canadian (Aboriginal) students translates into practical strategies for helping eliminate achievement gaps in diverse school communities.

He earned a master's degree in education administration and leadership studies and a bachelor's degree in secondary curriculum from the University of Victoria.

To learn about Charlie's work, visit him at www.heartofeducation.com.

Chris Weber, EdD, is a consultant and administrative coach for Chicago Public Schools and the Oakland (California) Unified School District. As principal of R. H. Dana Elementary School in the Capistrano Unified School District (CUSD) in California, Chris was the leader of a highly effective PLC. Together with his staff, he lifted the school to remarkable levels of success.

Designated Schoolwide Title I, with more than 60 percent of all students English learners and Latino and more than 75 percent socioeconomically disadvantaged, R.H. Dana consistently exceeded adequate yearly progress (AYP) goals. The school's gains over four years were among the top 1 percent in the state, and it was the first school in the decades-long history of the CUSD to win the State of California's Title I Academic Achievement Award. Under Chris's leadership, R. H. Dana earned the first California Distinguished School Award in the school's 42-year history. After the percentage of students meeting AYP in English and math tripled in four years, the school was named a National Blue Ribbon School. Chris credits these achievements to the daily practice of key principles: (1) focusing on student engagement, (2) maximizing instructional time, (3) reallocating resources, and (4) developing systematic student support programs based on response to intervention (RTI).

Chris has experience teaching grades K–12 and has served as a site administrator for elementary and secondary schools. He was director of instruction for the Garden Grove Unified School District in California, which was the 2004 winner of the prestigious Broad Prize for Urban Education. Chris led the district's 47 K–6 schools in helping all groups of students achieve double-digit AYP gains in mathematics and English language arts.

Chris is a coauthor of *Pyramid Response to Intervention: RTI, Professional Learning Communities, and How to Respond When Kids Don't Learn*. He also coauthored "The Why Behind RTI," the feature article in the October 2010 issue of *Educational Leadership*.

A graduate of the United States Air Force Academy and a former U.S. Air Force pilot, he holds a master's degree from California State University, San Marcos, and a doctorate of education from the University of California (Irvine and Los Angeles).

Follow Chris on Twitter @Chi_educate.

To book Tom, Charlie, or Chris for professional development, contact pd@solution-tree.com.

By Wayne Hulley

School improvement is a complex task. Ideally, it is an opportunity for educators to collaborate and grow professionally in the creation of schools that make a difference for all students. The reality, however, is that any school improvement process resulting in meaningful, lasting change is fraught with ambiguity and challenge. The improvement process in every school is unique, affected by demographics, existing culture, staff characteristics, and leadership. It is uneven and messy with many turns in the road and mountains to be climbed. The challenge resides in creating and sustaining a coordinated process for school improvement.

In this book, Tom, Charlie, and Chris have tried to simplify the complex. They believe that schools must create a positive learning environment in which both students and staff are inspired to do their best. To make this happen, they recommend a process with a focus on seven keys. Their research has shown that schools and classrooms that consistently bring this focus are able to have a significant impact on student learning and behavior. This book is built around common sense and the introduction of high-yield strategies, those things that we know help kids learn.

Many researchers have separated students' academic performance from their behavior. However, Tom, Charlie, and Chris believe it is possible, and preferable, for schools to work on both in a coordinated way. They have combined professional learning community (PLC) concepts with elements from positive behavioral interventions and support (PBIS) to create a system in which teachers work collaboratively to support both the learning and the behavioral needs of students—a system in which tremendous differences can occur. They share numerous examples from real schools that show the results that are possible when both types of student needs—learning and behavioral—are the focus.

Most teachers are already doing the best they can and are working hard to make a difference for students. To help these busy teachers, Tom, Charlie, and Chris have reduced the necessary elements for creating a school culture that supports both student learning and behavior to seven key components. They have discovered that these key components exist in schools and classrooms that are having a significant positive influence on students. The seven key components are about bringing a focus to a school and a classroom. They lead to the development of common expectations shared by all staff, targeted instruction in the areas needing improvement, and the creation of structures and strategies to provide appropriate support.

As someone who has struggled to make sense of school improvement for more than forty years, I found that this book not only highlights the key issues, but more importantly, it offers a sensible approach to confronting these issues. School improvement will never be easy, because it forces schools and teachers to change their behaviors. However, with constructive and proven strategies, school staff can make a positive difference. As Tom, Charlie, and Chris believe, the solution lies not in changing the students we have coming to our schools, but in changing our approach to working with them.

I highly recommend this book to those who care deeply about teaching and the future.

This We Believe

Education has changed. The job we are asked to do today is not the same job we were asked to do a decade ago. The focus has changed from *learning for some* to *learning for all*, and then to *learning for all, whatever it takes*. The stakes and expectations are higher than ever before. How can we reach such high expectations? Consider the traditional approach taken with an elementary student, Adam, who exhibits problem behaviors.

> Patricia, a third-grade teacher, is doing all she can to survive the "Year of Adam." Her disposition improves as the months pass, and she realizes that soon Adam will be passed on to fourth grade. John, the fourth-grade teacher, has heard all the negative feedback about Adam just prior to school closing for the break and now experiences the "Summer of Adam" as he counts down the days until the school year begins, losing sleep as the summer days slip away.

> Imagine, instead, if John had approached Adam before the summer break to greet him and let him know he would be his new teacher, providing some words of encouragement. Perhaps John even takes an interest in Adam and gathers some information about him. Adam likes the newest sports trading cards, so John gets a few packs to use during the school year. During the summer, John plans a "chance" encounter to let Adam know he is looking forward to the upcoming school year. On the opening day of school, all teachers have a number of items to hand out and review. John asks Adam to hand out some of the papers.

Some might argue that this example of how to motivate a student is too simple and naïve. However, we know what the traditional approach would produce. Remember, behavior occurs for one of two reasons: to get something or to avoid something. To change student behavior requires that we change our approach. There are countless opportunities to motivate students. And yet too often, we miss these opportunities.

The Best Kids

Charlie was sitting with a group of teachers during a lunch break one day, and the discussion quickly turned to confessing the sins of their students. In the confines of the staff room, teachers will sometimes vent frustrations by competing for the "worst student" story. It's a dangerous game to play because by repeating the stories, we can start to believe that most of our kids are bad. In fact, the opposite is true. Most of our kids are good, and they all have potential. Listening to the teachers, Charlie was reminded of a comment Wayne Hulley made during a presentation. "Parents," he said, "are sending us the best kids they have." The impact of the statement hit Charlie hard then, and it was reaffirmed as the teachers talked. Education embodies learning, growth, and improvement. We must work with the kids who show up to our classes every day. Parents are not keeping the really good ones at home and seeing how we do with the weaker ones first. There are no throwaway kids or designated failures. There are just students at different stages of learning. Education is not a random event. Teachers must stand before their classes with a firm and rooted belief that *every* student can be successful.

Every student has the potential to be successful. We need to unlock that potential in our most challenging students and point them in the direction most likely to produce the greatest chance for success. This is a personal journey for each student and cannot be accomplished by taking a one-size-fits-all approach to education. Instead, as DuFour, DuFour, Eaker, and Many (2010) describe, it must be a "whatever it takes" approach. There is too much at stake.

The Best Adults

The behavior and commitment of adult role models are critical to the success of any school improvement plan. Malcolm Gladwell (2009), in a summary of teacher effectiveness research, clearly showed that the difference between good teachers and poor teachers is vast. If we are to be successful in making a difference in the lives of kids, then we must model what we want to see. If we want our students and our school community to improve, change, grow, and learn, then *we* must be willing to change and improve. DuFour, DuFour, and Eaker (2008) refer to this as *collective commitment*:

> When educators clarify and commit to certain shared values, they are engaged in the essential ABCs of school improvement—identifying the actions, behaviors, and commitments necessary to bring mission and vision to life. (p. 148)

How we conduct ourselves, the choices we make, and the behaviors we model will be reflected back by our students. Gladwell (2009) estimates that the difference in student learning between a good teacher and an average teacher is equal to a year's worth of learning in a single year of school. According to Gladwell (2009), "Your child is actually better off in a bad school with an excellent teacher than in an excellent school with a bad teacher" (p. 317).

If our goal is to have all students learn and grow, we must begin to make a difference at the most basic levels first. Student behavior is key. The research on effective schools (Hulley & Dier, 2008; Lezotte, 1997) points to the importance of safe, orderly, and caring school environments. At the schoolwide level, there must be plans and systems in place to support a positive learning environment. Plans and systems are only as good as the people implementing them. Adult behavior must demonstrate commitment to the plan. At the classroom level, that safe environment starts with the teacher.

Brain-based research supports this notion that students learn very little academically if their social-emotional needs are not met first. It gets right back to Abraham Maslow's (1954) hierarchy of basic needs: we must feel safe and cared for before we can effectively concentrate on higher-level thinking. It does not matter how knowledgeable the teacher is about her subject area if she does not make an emotional connection with her students. It does not matter how well the teacher has planned his lesson if he has not created a safe, caring environment in his classroom. This point is emphasized by the high school senior who told us, "I want to get to know my teacher, and I want my teacher to know me."

Teacher Impact

Everyone seems to have at least one teacher that they remember fondly as having made a difference in their lives. Can you remember one? Stop for a moment and think about one of those high-impact teachers. What qualities did he or she possess? What did that teacher do to make a connection with you? How did that teacher make your learning meaningful? What impact did he or she have on your life?

When we ask this question at staff development sessions in any district, in any jurisdiction, the answers tend to cluster around several main themes. The themes most frequently cited are that the most memorable teacher:

- Cared about me as an individual
- Brought learning to life, made it real
- Took extra time to help me learn
- Was always fair, reasonable, and understanding
- Inspired me to do my best

Notice how these themes focus very little on the specialized knowledge of the teacher or the kind and number of tests and worksheets. Robyn Jackson (2009) notes, "Knowing your students means more than knowing their demographics or test scores" (p. 30). Memorable, high-impact teachers make a difference in the lives of students, one kid at a time.

Unfortunately, most adults can also think of at least one teacher who made their learning miserable. When we ask this question at workshops and seminars, common themes also emerge. In this category, the most prevalent themes are that the low-impact teacher:

- Did not know me or care about me
- Made the subject material dry and boring

- Was often unfair or arbitrary

- Yelled and screamed, put kids down, and belittled students

- Seemed more interested in the subject than the kids

We don't teach subjects, we teach kids! If the role of the teacher were to simply disseminate facts and mark assignments, it would be much more efficient doing nothing more than online correspondence. The advances in technology have rendered this dissemination of information a moot point. Those who reminisce for the good old days are thinking of life B.G.—before Google! Today's students have quicker and easier access to information than at any previous point in education. We are no longer the fonts of knowledge. Students can gather the knowledge in numerous ways and from a variety of sources. Our roles have shifted to helping students connect the knowledge into usable chunks of information that align with their passion and future pursuits. School is more than a fact-distribution center. Schools should be social places where students and staff learn together. The goal is to become a community of learners, where students develop socially and emotionally as well as academically. Teachers who do this very well or very poorly both leave a lasting legacy on many students.

Parents, teachers, support staff, and principals should be asking themselves these questions:

- In which category do I fall? Do I have high impact and inspire, or do I have low impact and demotivate my students?

- What am I doing to ensure that students get more positives and fewer negatives?

- Do I make a difference? How do I know?

Those of us who work in schools have a tremendous opportunity to impact the lives of so many kids. An elementary teacher over the course of her thirty-year career can make close personal connections with almost 1,000 kids in her care. A middle or high school teacher can come in direct contact with up to 200 or 300 kids per year, or upwards of 9,000 kids over a thirty-year career. We touch the lives of enough people to build whole villages or small towns. Collectively we build a nation. The real joy of this profession lies not in predicting the future, but in creating it.

The question is, what kinds of villages and towns are we building? How do we impact those students' lives? What do we model for them? What do we teach them? What life lessons do we leave them with? Referring to the following Haim Ginott (1976) quote, do we make the lives of those students miserable or joyous? What kind of community do we create?

> I have come to a frightening conclusion. I am the decisive element in the classroom. It is my personal approach that creates the climate. It is my daily mood that makes the weather. As a teacher I possess tremendous power

to make a child's life miserable or joyous. I can be a tool of humor, hurt or heal. In all situations it is my response that decides whether a crisis will be escalated or de-escalated, and a child humanized or de-humanized. (p. 13)

Community Building

It's easy to get sidetracked. There are so many demands on the individual teacher and principal. More requirements and expectations come down from politicians and departments of education. These get filtered through local school boards, superintendents, and directors of instruction and are then passed down again to those on the front lines. The adults in the building, who really just want to work with kids, are expected to add the new demands and expectations to already full and busy weeks, months, and years. This often distracts us from our core purpose, which is student learning.

Each one of these new demands has, at its heart, a serious intention to improve the school system for kids. However, such intentions often get lost in translation or buried in bureaucratic red tape. What begins as a good idea for kids and schools often becomes so onerous that it actually detracts from what educators do best—work with kids.

A case in point was an exercise one school district had to go through, an exercise in which an external review team visited schools across the district to give a report card of sorts.

Each school had to have its own School Planning Council (consisting of parents, teachers, and the principal), which was charged with the task of creating a "School Plan for Student Achievement," complete with measurable goals and a host of structures and strategies to support the plan. To be sure, this was very important stuff.

As the parents, teachers, principal, and support staff struggled to complete the document, they got bogged down in details and jargon, data, and evidence. This is not to say that all of these things are not important—they are. They are especially important when the goal is to improve student learning. But it is easy to lose sight of the forest because of our attention on every tree.

As the school team toiled over the details of the new plan, one of the parents on the School Planning Council reminded them of what this was all supposed to be about. She said, "It's simple. Safe, happy kids will learn. Our school plan needs to reflect that. It should be that simple."

That really is what it's all about. How we achieve that might look a little different in every school in every province or state. After you get past all the educational jargon and all the data crunching of test scores and letter grades, it comes down to creating a positive school environment.

Real-Estate Test

When discussing community building in staff development sessions, we often refer to the real-estate test. At some point in time, the house beside you will come up for sale. If the option were yours, who would you want to buy that house and become your neighbor? The reality is that the choice of buyer will come down to who meets (or beats) the list price. Think of some of the students who have been marginalized by the school system. Based on how the individual was treated as a student, will you be comfortable having him or her as your neighbor when he or she grows up to be an adult? Eventually, students become adults. Have you helped them to become the kind of people you want living on your street, or working at the garage and fixing your car, or cooking at the local restaurant and preparing your meal, or coming back to school and teaching *your* kids?

Success Is Individual

We want all kids to succeed. Success, however, is relative. How we measure success depends on how we view the situation. Whether we are talking about behavior or academics in school, success should be measured individually. As Alfie Kohn (2005) points out, "Kids who have an underlying sense of their own value are more likely to see failure as a temporary set-back, a problem to be solved" (p. 20). In an era of accountability, it is easy to get forced into a false sense of security from number crunching. Data are important, but simple, impersonal, standardized scores do not tell the whole story. We have to make meaning from government-initiated standardized tests in a way that makes sense for the students in our schools. If we are to be effective advocates for kids, we also have to have other, more personalized, individualized, meaningful data. Data are evidence of progress. We need personalized evidence to know and to show that we are making a difference for each individual child. For example, Horner, Sugai, and Todd (2001) suggest that if we look at behavior support for students, "information is needed about both individual students and the entire student body" (p. 20). To do that, we have to start by knowing where the student is now. Only then will we be able to celebrate successes when we can show that there has been improvement. This is true for both behavior and academics.

In the final term of the year, a number of students in Mrs. Hart's and Mrs. Gold's grade 8 classes had stopped attending regularly and were in danger of not passing the term (and possibly the year). By the last two weeks of classes, the teachers were very worried that these six or seven students would not pass, as they were falling further and further behind in their learning with each day of school that they missed. In an effort to make sure that these students were able to show their learning (and pass grade 8), Mrs. Hart and Mrs. Gold put together a folder for each of these at-risk learners containing assignments that, while slightly adapted, would meet the major learning outcomes for the term. When these particular learners arrived at school, Mrs. Hart or Mrs. Gold offered them the chance to catch up on all their learning and pass grade 8 in as much time as it took them to complete all of the major outcomes of the term (organized in an easy-to-understand way in the folders).

When the students understood what was being offered to them (a chance to finish grade 8 in less than two weeks), and accepted the responsibility of this deal (working through the folder of learning all day long, at the back of Mrs. Gold's classroom and forgoing all classroom activities and lessons), they were asked to call their parents to get permission. Students knew that when they were able to show that they had learned all of the major outcomes, they were officially finished with grade 8 and did not have to return to classes.

Because attendance was a major struggle for most of these learners, a few of them did not show up at school in those last two weeks, and they did not pass grade 8. Three of the students, though, happened to arrive at school on the Monday that Mrs. Hart and Mrs. Gold planned to begin this program. Armed with the folders, textbooks, calculators, paper, pencils, granola bars, and juice boxes, Mrs. Gold was able to keep them in her room without giving them any excuses to leave. After just one day of successfully completing a number of learning outcomes, all three students showed up three or four days in a row (an attendance run that none of them had met since early in Term 2), and were able to walk out the doors of the school, feeling successful, a full week earlier than their peers. One other student, Colton, did not have attendance problems, but was on an IEP for his learning disability, and took medication for attention deficit disorder.

As the end of the year drew closer and closer, Colton was having tremendous difficulty staying focused on his learning. Mrs. Hart and Mrs. Gold offered him the same deal as they had offered the other three learners, and Colton was able to finish all of his grade 8 learning in just two school days (and a weekend, as he took some work home with him). He, too, walked out of school a few days before his peers, feeling successful, and, in his own words, "Responsible, like it's my own choice to do this."

Goal Setting

Every school is different, and every student unique, but most of us in schools have a similar long-term goal. Parents and educators want students to graduate and become successful, contributing members of society.

We have a clear understanding of our long-term goal; the challenge is the short-term goals that will lead to our desired long-term reality. Building small successes along the way and celebrating them often will contribute to our long-term success. Celebrations are great community-creators and culture-builders. As Bolman and Deal (2002) state, celebration and ceremony "are antidotes to boredom, cynicism, and burnout. They bring members of a group together, strengthen bonds, and build spirit and faith" (p. 104).

Long-term plans, mission statements, vision statements, and values and beliefs proclamations are all important aspects of a sustainable learning organization (Senge, 1990). However, we have found that it is equally important to celebrate short-term successes. This helps people in the organization quickly see that their efforts are making a difference. In his landmark book *The 7 Habits of Highly Effective People*, Steven Covey (1989) identifies a key habit as being able to "begin with the end in mind." Having goals and celebrating the steps along the way provides tangible evidence to individuals and groups that their daily efforts are paying off. This is motivating and helps to generate momentum toward the longer-term goals (Schmoker, 1999).

The premise is quite simple and is based on the following ideas:

1. Schools are important and good.

2. Schools can, should, and must provide a safe, caring, and positive environment in which to learn.

3. Schools must systematically create opportunities for success for *all* learners.

Relationships

If effective teaching had to be summarized in one word, that word would be *relationships*. Creating and managing effective relationships is the core skill required by all educators. It sets the tone for the entire school year and the time beyond, when we no longer have as direct an impact on students. It lies in the routines, practices, and expectations we have for our students, our parents, our peers, and our other education partners.

Picture the classroom in which the teacher has a rule about homework completion. If the rule is "no homework, no mark," then it is simple to enforce. At the start of the class, the teacher asks all students to take out their work and circulates around the room checking the work. The situation collapses when the teacher stops at the desk of a noncompliant student and lectures about not completing homework. The lecture extends to reminders of the number of times homework has not been completed by this student and culminates with a reference to the older sibling of the student who also did not complete homework. Even the most patient student would lose his or her cool at this point.

Imagine, instead, that the teacher adheres to the rule and simply records the lack of completion. After the class has started and students are working individually, the teacher approaches the student and works privately with him on the previous assignment or makes plans to do so. In this instance, the student opens up to reveal some concern about the assignment. A relationship is fostered instead of being destroyed. The message to the rest of the class is that everyone matters.

Long after many of the other skills we teach students have become dormant, the quality of our relationships will endure. When you think about your time in school, it is more likely that you will recall an individual than a content piece. Consider the following story.

A teacher, Mike, and his family had completed the first leg of their Christmas vacation and were looking forward to getting home. As they reached the terminal where they would be making the transfer for their final flight home, they were advised that weather conditions would prevent them from flying and that they would be taking a bus for five hours. As they boarded the bus, the airline employee who had been helping organize the ground transportation called out the teacher's name. He then asked the question every educator dreads: "Do you remember me?" As Mike struggled through his memory bank, the employee sensed his difficulty and offered his name. They spoke for a bit, and the employee indicated he had something he had wanted to share for some time. "Do you remember when you used to open the gym up for floor hockey on Friday nights?" he asked. Mike did recall this activity and his own reasons for doing it. The employee went on to say that he and a number of his friends used to engage in heavy drinking every Friday night. Mike opening the gym gave him an excuse to pass on the drinking. He would tell his friends that he had made a commitment to Mike to show up.

Mike couldn't recall if his former student had been a good athlete or not. That didn't matter. What mattered was that the former student became a successful adult who remembered how important that activity was for him. Although Mike considered himself to be a good teacher, the former student didn't recall any of the magic Mike thought he brought to his lessons—only what Mike did to build the relationship.

All students need to know they have people they can turn to at school. Oftentimes, the significant adult is their main or homeroom teacher. It may be another teacher in the school, any of the support staff, someone in the office, or their coach. Never underestimate the powerful influence of a supportive adult. The support may be just a moment taken to produce a smile, listen to a story, or provide an alternate choice. It does not have to be the lesson being taught that day. More often, those less structured moments offer our greatest chance to make a connection. The reality is that we create those less structured moments by ensuring that in our structured times we present ourselves as being focused on kids and available to assist them as they mature.

The McCreary Centre Society surveys students in grades 7–12 on a variety of youth issues. One of its surveys (McCreary Centre Society, 2003) looked at youth who feel connected to school and how this relates to risk behaviors. The information is summarized in figure I.1 (page 10) and shows a significant difference between high and low levels of school connectedness.

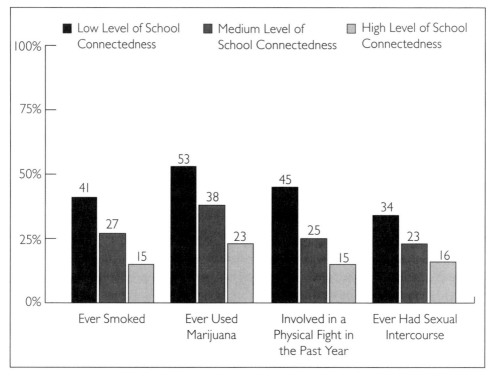

Figure I.1: School connectedness and risk behaviors.

The groundwork for establishing these important relationships lies in positively interacting with our students. This requires educators to actively supervise and circulate around the class. It is important that we catch kids being good and notice their positive contributions. This does not mean that we should avoid the rule violations that occur from time to time. It suggests that we follow a rule correction with positive reinforcement when the behavior is the desired one. In order to maximize our time on positive outcomes, we must arrive prepared for the class, have clear expectations of outcome and objectives, check frequently for understanding, and engage students in activities.

A Simple, Systematic Approach

In the rest of this book, we present the seven keys to a positive learning environment. One might conclude that these seven keys represent simply a systematic approach to building relationships. We'd agree. Further, we'd argue that therein lies another reason why creating and sustaining systems of behavioral supports is essential, foundational work for schools. Educating youth is challenging and critically important to society. What will have the biggest impact on our success? What are the biggest obstacles to achieving our goals? What does research suggest is a fundamental aspect of our efforts? We propose that establishing positive learning environments—collaboratively created, systematically sustained—is focused, powerful work that every school should consider.

one

Creating a Positive Learning Environment

Behavior and academic achievement are inextricably linked. A student's academic success in school is directly related to the student's attention, engagement, and behavior. The higher the expectation for scholarly behaviors and the better the supports for students experiencing difficulties—whether mild, moderate, or severe—the more academic success can be achieved.

— Austin Buffum, Mike Mattos, and Chris Weber

This claim by Buffum, Mattos, and Weber (2009, p. 111) is a call to action for educators across North America as we respond to the challenges we face in educating students in the 21st century. We believe that academic and behavioral performance go hand in hand. One study (Hawkins, Catalano, Kosterman, Abbott, & Hill, 1999) found that when schools raised their level of academic achievement, behavior problems decreased—and when schools worked to decrease behavior problems, academic achievement improved.

We must focus on these two foundational pieces—academic achievement and behavior—if we are to promote success for all students. Moreover, we must do so while facing the challenges we encounter as educators through collaborative, cooperative work with our colleagues—the practice of professional learning communities (PLCs). We acknowledge that this practice is one to which we must continually commit.

We do make a difference. As educators, we have to believe that statement. Every child who enters our classrooms at the start of a school year will be different by the end of that school year. The question is, how will our students change? By the end of the academic year, will they simply be one year older? Will they simply have a year's worth of new facts in their heads? Will students merely spew back the facts we want to hear, or will they be independent thinkers, mature enough to tackle the academic and social challenges ahead of them? The answers to these questions come from the actions of the adults within a school. What we do with students and how we do it, from the beginning to the end of the school year, are critical. The research (Barth, 2006; Fullan, 2005) on school improvement is clear—it is the shared experience and common approach to addressing emerging and evident needs of our students that will move us forward.

To be effective in helping all students learn, the adults in a school must come to agreement on what is most important. We must have crucial conversations about what we believe about how students learn. We must collaboratively establish norms regarding how we will work and learn together. Collectively, we need to commit to common expectations for both student and adult behavior. We need to ask:

- What are our common expectations for how students behave?

- What are our common expectations for how staff work and interact? What about parents and other community members?

- What do we know about best-practice and high-yield strategies that make a difference in student learning?

- What collective commitments will we make to ensure that the very highest levels of adult and student behavior become a reality in our school?

The answers to these questions create the foundation for moving a school forward.

As the focus on collaboration in these questions suggests, effective teaching is not a solo act. Robert Marzano (2003, 2007) and DuFour et al. (2010) clearly illustrate that collaborative planning, collective inquiry, and shared commitments enhance the effectiveness of both teaching and learning. Whether we look at behavior, discipline, attendance, or academics, schools that operate as PLCs have the best chance to measurably improve student performance (Buffum et al., 2009).

PLCs ensure that all students have access to a quality education. It is not enough to be satisfied with the success of students who are easy to reach and easy to teach. As educators, we have a fundamental responsibility to support the individual and collective needs of all students. Our schools are no longer built on the premise of learning for some; rather, we now focus on learning for all. We have similarly advanced from learning for overall subgroups to learning for every single child. This commitment is documented in legislation such as the Individuals with Disabilities Education Improvement Act (IDEIA, 2004) and similar initiatives in most states and provinces. Response to intervention (RTI), a key component of the reauthorization of IDEIA, represents a philosophy and framework for ensuring that every student receives the support he or she needs to be successful.

Legislation, however, is relatively easy to craft; it is more difficult to ensure that this philosophy and framework become a practical reality in schools and classrooms. Our students come to us with challenges that are different from those of previous generations, and they face unique challenges for their futures.

Educators must make a commitment to approach these challenges in a positive way, by helping students find their passion as they prepare for a world vastly different from the one we faced. We cannot change the students who come into our schools; rather, we must change our approach to working with them. We must commit to proactively serving students by anticipating their needs. We can predict that students will experience frustration, confusion, and perhaps failure in the absence of clearly articulated routines, structures, and expectations for their learning environment. This book will help teachers and school leaders transform the research on student behavior into practical realities for superior school and classroom climates and cultures in which learning is primed to occur.

Over the years, as we have worked with many staffs in a number of school districts, our repertoire of strategies for improving student behavior and overall educational effectiveness has evolved. While there can be no complete, exhaustive list of strategies for making a difference with students, we hope that those presented in this book will help you and your school community get to a place where staff, students, and community members can answer "Yes!" to the following ten questions (Hierck, 2009a):

1. Does everyone in our school agree on why we are here?
2. Does everyone really believe we can make a difference for all kids?
3. In terms of making a difference, do we have a common schoolwide vision?
4. Are clear and specific schoolwide systems in place to make our vision a reality?
5. Are classroom plans in place that match the schoolwide systems?
6. Are individual student support options in place?
7. Do procedures in the office support the school, classroom, and individual plans?
8. Does every adult talk about these plans openly, regularly, and systematically?
9. Do we know, with measurable evidence, that the plans are making a difference?
10. If our plans are not making a difference, are we willing to try something new?

In an era of educational accountability in which the public demands increasing levels of student safety and academic achievement, it is imperative that we find ways to create positive learning environments. Educators can have an incredible impact on the young people in their classrooms. It is both an awesome responsibility and a fantastic opportunity. The most successful educational institutions are those that create conditions for deep and meaningful learning. Schools that focus on the needs of students, enlist the shared expertise of educators, and invite parents to participate have the best chance of creating a positive learning environment.

This book describes seven key components that, in our experience, improve the conditions for learning in any school: (1) common expectations, (2) targeted instruction, (3) positive reinforcement, (4) support strategies and interventions, (5) collaborative teams, (6) data-driven dialogue, and (7) a schoolwide systems approach. Throughout this book, we share real-life examples of schools making a difference with kids by using the seven key components. We support these seven key components with current research, especially the work around effective schools, PLCs, and positive behavioral interventions and supports (PBIS). The seven key components help pull these powerful, proven school improvement strategies together in a realistic and doable way. As effective schools expert Wayne Hulley notes in his foreword, this book is built around "high-yield strategies, those things that we know help kids learn."

The Pyramid of Behavior

Before we can do the hard work of improving student behavior, we need to have a firm understanding of effective classroom management and a positive schoolwide climate. Students need to feel safe at school, educators need to feel supported in their efforts to create a safe place to learn, and parents need to feel secure that school really is a safe place for their children.

The behavior pyramid (figure 1.1) is a helpful tool to examine how behavior issues are dispersed throughout a school population and what structures need to be in place to deal with them. It shows the typical breakdown of behavior issues within a student population. The challenge for educators is to remember to look at the whole pyramid and avoid the trap of focusing only on the problems at the top. And we must remember that, when it comes to changing patterns of behavior, if we can predict it, we can prevent it.

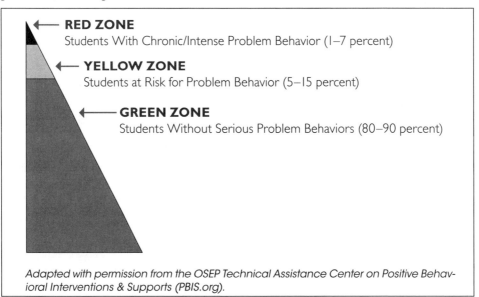

RED ZONE
Students With Chronic/Intense Problem Behavior (1–7 percent)

YELLOW ZONE
Students at Risk for Problem Behavior (5–15 percent)

GREEN ZONE
Students Without Serious Problem Behaviors (80–90 percent)

Adapted with permission from the OSEP Technical Assistance Center on Positive Behavioral Interventions & Supports (PBIS.org).

Figure 1.1: The pyramid of behavior.

The pyramid has three zones—green, yellow, and red. The bottom of the pyramid is the solid base. This "green zone" is where the majority of students in our schools reside. These students are easy to reach and easy to teach. The middle group on the pyramid represents 5 percent to 10 percent of a student population. Sugai and Horner (2006) refer to these students as being in the "yellow zone." These students may be a challenge to teach but easy to reach, or vice versa. The tip of the pyramid represents 1 percent to 7 percent of students in a school. Sugai and Horner (2006) refer to these students as being in "the red zone." These are the students who might be identified as being a challenge to teach and reach. Next, we will examine each zone of the pyramid and look at how positive behavioral intervention works in each zone.

The Green Zone

The green zone is made up of students who help the school run smoothly. These students not only passively follow the rules, but they also model appropriate behaviors and directly and indirectly moderate less-than-appropriate behaviors. This modeling of appropriate behaviors helps set a positive tone in the school. It is critically important to acknowledge the green zone students and their contributions; however, educators should not get wrapped up in expecting every student to be in this group. Many of our teachable moments happen in motivating students in the yellow and red zones to move toward the green zone. We need to make it clear to students that the green zone is an attractive place to be.

The Yellow Zone

We often refer to students in this middle zone of behavior as the *wannabes*, because they want to be where they perceive the action to be. Students in this yellow zone may misbehave when adults are not present, or when a critical mass of students in the green zone is not present. This is an important group to watch, and it may become the measure of success for schools. Schools may never eliminate the top of the pyramid. The reality is that red zone students will always be there, and ensuring their success will require individualized, creative, ever-evolving supports. However, it is possible to shrink the yellow zone. These students require more attention than those in the green zone, but the investment consistently pays off. Positive peer pressure from students in the green zone can moderate infrequent misbehavior from students in the yellow zone, and staff can often predict and prevent misbehavior by these students.

The Red Zone

Students in the red zone present the most significant challenge to educators. These are the students who present the most disrupting and difficult behavior, act out the most often, and require the most structured interventions. These students tend to display multiple infractions of school rules. The inappropriate behavior of this small group tends to be more frequent and more intense than the majority of students. Schools can decrease the number of students in the red zone; however, students who remain may have unpredictable behaviors that require constant reinforcements and corrections.

Students in the red zone are entitled to the same educational experiences and opportunities as the rest of the student population. Traditional responses to red zone behavior have been various forms of exclusion, such as removing a student to the back or side of a classroom, into the hallway or another classroom, to the office, or to in-school or out-of-school suspension. Interestingly, to avoid the paperwork and stigmas associated with suspensions, at times parents are simply asked to take a student home for the rest of the day. However, as Lane and Murakami (1987) conclude, although exclusion is the most common response for youth with conduct disorders, juvenile delinquency, and disordered behavior, research shows this type of punishment is associated with "increased aggression, vandalism, truancy, tardiness, and dropping out" (Sulzer-Azaroff & Mayer, 1991).

This deliberate action by educators to deny students in the red zone with educational opportunities runs contrary to the basic definition of education (and to federal IDEIA legislation); we are essentially taking those students with the smallest skill set and working to reduce it even further by denying them educational outcomes necessary for successful functioning in adult life. The fewer experiences and opportunities these students have while growing up, the more limited their adult opportunities become and the greater the likelihood they will become incarcerated or permanent, unemployed fixtures of their neighborhood. Consider the following research findings.

Walker, Colvin, and Ramsey (1995) found that three years after leaving school, 70 percent of youth identified as antisocial while at school had been arrested. When combined with their work showing that aggression is as stable over time as intelligence, the authors paint a bleak picture of the future for youth who have been abandoned by the educational system.

Dishion and Patterson (1997) identify factors in the home that contribute to antisocial behavior and cite inconsistent management, reactive discipline, and lack of monitoring as key factors. The model of the 1950s nuclear family with a single wage earner being able to fully support the family is rare. In its place, we often find parents harried by work, with minimal time for family.

Biglan (1995) cites factors in the community that contribute to antisocial behavior among youths and lists antisocial networks of peers and the lack of prosocial engagement as keys. Healthy communities have many opportunities for their youth to participate in activities. In the absence of these, children gather and engage in less desirable activities.

While we cannot be responsible for eradicating all the factors that lead students to choose negative behavior, we can seek to understand them and attempt to manage those over which we have control, which will contribute to a more positive and productive school environment.

When using this pyramid approach, we need to be careful about how we describe the tiers and the students within them. The green zone, yellow zone, and red zone are broad generalizations of behavior, not permanent labels attached to any student. The zones are helpful when thinking about the school population as a whole, to remind us that the largest group of students is doing the right thing most of the time. Further, if we believe educators make a difference for kids, then we must also believe that students can move from red and yellow zone behavior to green zone behavior. Our role is to support and facilitate that transition.

Response to intervention (RTI) promotes this idea with its focus on a three-tiered approach to intervention (Tier 1, Tier 2, and Tier 3). In RTI, students in the top tier receive the most intensive interventions. Students with special needs are general education students first and always (President's Commission on Excellence in Special Education, 2002). The support given in the pyramid of behavior model is identical to the academic support associated with RTI. All students, including those with special needs, receive high-quality core intervention. Tiered supports are then provided to all students, including those identified as having a disability, based on their specific needs, not based on a general label.

Clear expectations, appropriate modifications, and consistency are the hallmarks for working with all students, especially students in the red zone. Figure 1.2 shows how students in all three zones receive increasingly intense levels of intervention (primary, secondary, and tertiary). We will address these interventions later in this chapter when we present the seven keys to a positive learning environment, and then in each subsequent chapter throughout the remainder of this book.

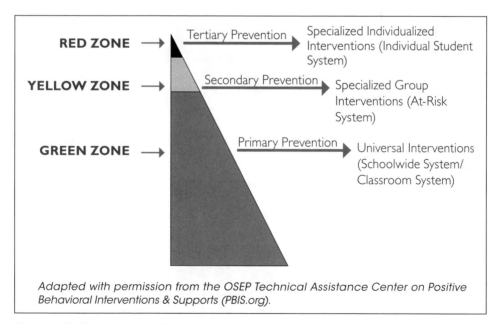

Adapted with permission from the OSEP Technical Assistance Center on Positive Behavioral Interventions & Supports (PBIS.org).

Figure 1.2: The pyramid of behavior.

The Seven Keys

The seven keys to a positive learning environment bring together the multi-tiered approach of positive behavioral support and interventions as described in the pyramid of behavior with many of the concepts of the PLC and PBIS approaches to school improvement (see figure 1.3). These two well-researched school improvement initiatives, when combined, become a powerful tool that can be used to create a positive learning environment in any school.

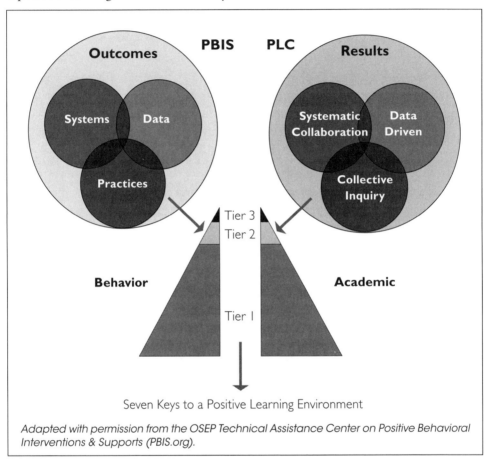

Seven Keys to a Positive Learning Environment

Adapted with permission from the OSEP Technical Assistance Center on Positive Behavioral Interventions & Supports (PBIS.org).

Figure 1.3: PBIS, PLC, and the seven keys to a positive learning environment.

PBIS focuses on behavior, while PLCs emphasize academic learning. However, both require a systematic, schoolwide approach to improvement. We created the graphic in figure 1.3 to illustrate this connection. The end result for both approaches is improved student outcomes, and both require the collaborative efforts of the adults in the school. Let's take a closer look at the similarities:

- PBIS promotes a focus on measurable outcomes, and PLCs focus on results.

- PBIS emphasizes using measurable data, and PLCs promote data-driven inquiry.

- PBIS encourages the use of research-validated teaching practices, and PLCs encourage learner-focused action research on best practices.

- PBIS is structured around systematic analysis by a school-based team, and PLCs are structured around systematic team collaboration.

- Both recommend targeted intervention structured within a tiered system of increasingly intensive interventions.

- The pyramid of interventions for both PBIS and PLC start with global, schoolwide prevention at the general classroom level (Tier 1) and increase in intensity to small-group (Tier 2) and one-on-one (Tier 3) interventions as determined by data and student need.

These two initiatives are clearly very similar in their structure and intent. Working with many schools across North America, it has been our experience that successful implementation of PBIS really requires a "behavior PLC." As Buffum et al. (2009) note in their description of principal Anthony Muhammad's impressive success at Glen Levey Middle School, "Until the school created a safe, orderly campus that addressed students' social and emotional needs, it could not address their academic needs" (p. 122).

It is our assertion that successful implementation of PBIS and PLCs is enhanced by focusing on these seven keys (Coleman, 2003, pp. 7–8):

1. Common expectations

2. Targeted instruction

3. Positive reinforcement

4. Support strategies and interventions

5. Collaborative teams

6. Data-driven dialogue

7. Schoolwide systems approach

In the following sections, we briefly define these key components by explaining what they look like when successfully implemented. Chapters 2 through 6 present the strategies and tools to implement each component to create a positive learning environment.

Common Expectations

Successful schools condense school rules, codes of conduct, and mission statements into a few easy-to-remember, positive common words or phrases. They set a positive tone by linking behavior expectations to academic expectations. Students, staff, and parents know what the expectations are, and everyone in the school uses a common language. Adults in the school model the expectations. We discuss common expectations in chapter 2.

Targeted Instruction

In successful schools, all staff teach common schoolwide expectations in a variety of ways and in various settings (in classes, the library, during assemblies, on the bus, and so on) to all students. They give students opportunities to develop, practice, and demonstrate these appropriate social and academic skills. Staff members focus on common expectations and related social skills by reviewing them regularly, practicing them frequently, and recognizing and rewarding them when students display the skills correctly. They teach social skills in the same manner as academic skills, using a process of demonstrate, practice, review, and celebrate. We discuss targeted instruction in chapter 3.

Positive Reinforcement

In successful schools, all adults working with students make a conscious effort to "catch kids being good," both formally and informally, on a regular basis. This timely and specific feedback is critical to improved learning. Celebration, recognition, and reward systems honor students for demonstrating positive behavior and common expectations. School staff members who are uncomfortable with tokens and rewards can concentrate instead on acknowledging, honoring, and thanking students for displaying positive social and academic skills in less extrinsic ways. At a minimum, staff should agree to intentionally and systemically (in the same manner, with the same frequency, and for the same reasons) reinforce behaviors that they wish to see more commonly displayed—behaviors that contribute to positive learning environments in which all students learn at the very highest levels. We discuss positive reinforcement in chapter 3.

Support Strategies and Interventions

Successful schools have a written, proactive plan that provides a series of strategies staff can follow when dealing with student misbehavior. All staff know and follow the systematic plan. It includes a continuum of strategies to support staff as they work to improve students' individual and group behavior. The focus of the plan and strategies is to help students learn to behave and succeed in the classroom, but alternatives exist for escalating levels of misbehavior. Staff members acknowledge that special situations and special students (those students who do not respond to Tier 1 supports and require Tier 2 and 3 strategies and interventions) may require special and unique plans; they are prepared to treat students differently based on their needs, and they accept that equitable and equal are not the same. We discuss support strategies and interventions in chapter 4.

Collaborative Teams

When a student's behavior escalates, or academics become a significant concern, successful schools refer students to a school-based team. With parental involvement, the team develops an individual plan specific to the needs and challenges of the individual child. The plans might include observations, behavior data, and functional assessments (with training). Functional assessments help educators arrive at the reasons for misbehavior; they are typically completed by psychologists who have received specialized training. These plans are specific, observable, and measurable and include consistent follow-up. Successful staffs know when and how to access a school-based team for student academic and behavioral issues. A collaborative team for further diagnosing and prescribing behavior needs is a fundamental trait of this component, and every member of the staff behaves collaboratively, cooperatively, and is willing to compromise to help all students in all situations. In chapter 4, we provide some behavior analysis tools. We discuss collaborative teams in chapter 5.

Data-Driven Dialogue

Successful schools have systems for data collection in place to track schoolwide behavior and academic progress. Staff members acknowledge that the quality and quantity of data that are collected provide timely information about which students are committing what infractions, during what times of the day, and in which locations in order to better inform decision making at the school and individual levels. The information teams collect is specific enough to generate general baseline data, schoolwide trends, and patterns of behavior for individual students. The information is shared with staff and is used in proactive ways to adjust, modify, or reteach specific skills. It is also a source of information for recognizing and celebrating positive behavior and academic trends. We discuss data-driven dialogue and provide sample data collection tools in chapter 5.

Schoolwide Systems Approach

In successful schools, systems are in place to ensure a consistent approach to behavior throughout the whole school. Students, staff, and parents know how the system works. Administrators model high expectations, place priority on social skills, and catch kids being good. They also support staff and school-based team efforts and ensure that data-tracking systems are consistent and relevant. The schoolwide system is secure enough to withstand staff changes, yet flexible enough to accommodate changes in situations and circumstances as they arise.

Success Stories

We have seen measurable improvements in schools where we have worked to implement the seven keys to a positive learning environment. Consider the following examples*:

- Mountain Middle School, a large suburban school, went from 2,200 office referrals per year for behavior problems to 1,200 in just one year of implementation. When the staff was surveyed, 97 percent indicated that there was more positive behavior in the school. More important than the statistics for the staff was the improved academic tone in the school.

*All of the examples in this book come from our real work in schools across the United States and Canada. We have used fictitious names for many of the schools described in this book at the request of the administration.

Substitute teachers who had refused work at the middle school before the planned interventions were now willing to teach there again.

- In Henry Elementary, a large urban school in a big city, graffiti and gang recruitment were at least weekly occurrences. Through the implementation of a system of behavioral supports over the course of several years, and with parent participation and the leadership of a broad base of teachers, graffiti and gang activity disappeared and the percentage of students receiving proficient scores or above on state tests in mathematics and English language arts more than doubled.

- Orca Bay Elementary, a midsized semirural school, saw a consistent decrease in the number of students visiting the office for behavior problems. Over three years, the school went from 775 office referrals to 365. Prior to the planned interventions, more than 50 percent of the student population had visited the office for negative consequences. After two years of following this plan, only 30 percent of the students had to visit the office. Even more telling was the fact that only 17 percent were referred to the office more than once. Only 6 percent were referred more than three times. As discipline problems decreased, staff also noted an increased focus on academics and improved results.

- The staff of Johnson Secondary School, a large suburban high school, did not feel a great need to focus on behavior and social skills. Most staff members believed their job was to deliver curriculum and prepare students for final exams. Based on office referral data and issues referred to the counseling office, the counselors and administrators identified a need to address behavior and social skills. After a daylong session identifying roadblocks to greater academic success for students, most staff members acknowledged the connection between behavior and academics. To their surprise, their students readily accepted the new approach. One grade 12 student commented, "It's nice to be caught being good for a change, instead of only being noticed when you do something wrong." Students, in fact, took the approach even further, starting their own antiviolence and antiracism group called SAVE (Students Against Violence Everywhere). Staff and students surveyed later noted a positive improvement in school climate.

Undertaking the Challenge

As we conclude this introductory chapter, let's acknowledge a few facts that we may either conveniently overlook or too quickly assume are true. First, well-designed and well-implemented classroom management programs are absolutely fundamental in establishing positive and effective learning environments, and design and implementation are not easy. We must strive as educators to support one another and ensure that effective classroom management is systematic.

Next, positive relationships between students and adults matter and make a difference. Let's acknowledge that students with whom a few teachers may have difficulties are, at times, successful in other teachers' classes. The reason is often that the latter teachers place importance on relationships and have predictable, productive structures, routines, and procedures in place in their classrooms (Marzano, Marzano, & Pickering, 2003).

Finally, let's not simply assume that all staff will answer affirmatively, if they answer honestly, to the two non-negotiable questions that are foundational within a PLC (DuFour et al., 2010):

1. Do you believe all students can learn at high levels?

2. Are you willing to do whatever it takes to ensure that this occurs?

We hope, and perhaps too quickly assume, that all educators will answer not just affirmatively, but enthusiastically, to these two questions. Nothing will undermine the success of behavioral or academic systems of support quicker than staff who inconsistently or unfaithfully implement agreed-upon strategies and interventions because they do not believe all students can learn and teachers should do whatever it takes to make sure the learning happens. High expectations for all students and collaboration among the professionals within a school are not negotiable.

What can we do to make sure all staff share a common devotion to implementing the seven keys to a positive learning environment? We can allow all staff members to have a voice and express themselves, and then share the research and rationale for the strategies we choose to implement. Educators deserve to know why changes are necessary before they are mandated to implement them (Muhammad, 2009).

In the New York Times bestseller *Influencer: The Power to Change Anything*, Patterson, Grenny, Maxfield, McMillan, and Switzler (2008) note:

> Before you can influence change, you have to decide what you're trying to change. Influence geniuses focus on behaviors. They're universally firm on this point. They don't dive into developing influence strategies until they've identified the behaviors they want to change. (p. 23)

This leads us to the next chapter, Common Expectations, where we examine the first of the seven keys to a positive learning environment in more depth. We must establish with clarity the behaviors we will expect from students so that we can reinforce them consistently, recognize when expectations are met, and correct when expectations are missed and so that we, the adults, can model the behaviors always.

two

Common Expectations

The first component for developing a positive learning environment where the majority of students are in the green zone (or moving toward the green zone) is common expectations. Common expectations are positively phrased school rules, codes of conduct, and mission statements that link behavior expectations to academic expectations. Students, staff, and parents know what the expectations are, everyone in the school uses a common language to describe the expectations, and adults in the school model the expectations.

In *A Basic School: A Community for Learning*, Ernest Boyer (1995) writes of the difficulty we face when all stakeholders do not share expectations:

> School is, above all else, a *community for learning*, a place where staff and students, along with parents, have a shared vision of what the institution is seeking to accomplish. There is simply no way to achieve educational excellence in a school where purposes are blurred, where teachers and students fail to communicate thoughtfully with each other, and where parents are uninvolved in the education of their children. (p. 15)

It is not always easy to keep a focus on common expectations with the ebbs and flows all schools experience as they deal with staff changes and the annual influx of new students. One of the keys to maintaining common expectations is to have a system in place that is sustainable, regardless of the players in that system.

Efforts to produce long-term change require a commitment of energy and time from all stakeholders. Every stakeholder must be involved and willing to make a difference. Schools must be willing to ask the difficult questions: Is student misbehavior a result of difficulties between students? Or difficulties within families? Or difficulties within the community? Or could we, the adults and professionals in the schools, change some of our practices to improve student behavior? If there is not a solid rationale for continuing a practice, then staff must be willing to drop the practice and replace it with something more in tune with the school's vision.

In this chapter, we'll use the example of a vice principal, Mr. Jones, and his school, Wilson Middle School, to highlight the importance and realities of holding a school staff accountable to common expectations.

Wilson Middle School: Developing Common Expectations

New Vice Principal Jones faced many challenges as he prepared for the start of the school year at Wilson, a rural junior high school of 700 students. The previous year, the school hit bottom. Student unrest led to increases in almost every category of misbehavior. Staff dejection manifested itself in a "bunker mentality"—most staff were neither collaborating nor communicating nor striving to continuously improve; they were surviving, at least in a professional sense, from day to day. Parental disapproval and lack of support for the school and its programs resulted in widespread community disenchantment. The school was the subject of negative stories making the gossip rounds. Local real estate agents advised families against buying houses in the area. Many solutions were proposed, but all required somebody else to change. Finger pointing was rampant.

Pledging Commitment

Vice Principal Jones started on the path to improvement by establishing common expectations for all stakeholders through a series of meetings. Mr. Jones held initial meetings with individual staff members, and then consolidated the information and shared it in a whole-staff meeting. He held similar meetings with parents, students, and community members. This was not an easy process—it required teachers to let go of those strategies that they felt most comfortable with and to embrace new ones in the hopes that a better system would emerge. In a time when quick solutions were desired, Vice Principal Jones preached patience for the long term. Stakeholders pledged to hold firm on new agreements and to support the changes and encourage others during their struggles to adjust.

Identifying Expectations and Creating Procedures

Vice Principal Jones sought to create a schoolwide disciplinary approach to which all stakeholders would commit. Teachers would create their own approaches to handling disciplinary issues in their classrooms, but within defined parameters linked to the overarching school expectations. In approaching behavior this way, Vice Principal Jones wished to emphasize and preserve autonomy in the classroom. To this end, he invited teachers to create a three-step process for their classrooms. The following is an example of one teacher's plan:

1. Identify the student who is not following the rule: "Jill, remember that you need to raise your hand when you want to contribute to the discussion."

2. Write the student's name on the board, and provide a reference to the desired expectation: "Jill, remember the rule we discussed as a class."

3. Remove the student from the classroom into the classroom of another colleague in close proximity and provide work for the student: "Jill, I need you to gather your materials and follow me into the hallway."

Any further misbehavior in the new classroom resulted in a referral to the office and the teacher contacting the student's parents to engage them in a plan to change the student's behavior.

In the three-step process, teachers first identify the concern, then follow up with a specific action that highlights that a change in behavior is needed, and then follow with a consequence. In the example, the teacher ultimately provided the student with a break from the familiar classroom environment. This proved to be a powerful deterrent at Wilson, and cases of further acting out in the school were quite minimal. Students whose misbehavior is caused by academic challenges can be redirected to a space that allows for their needs to be met—for example, in a room where an intervention teacher can support them.

Implementing Procedures

The vice principal kept each teacher's three-step process on file in the office so each teacher's approach would be familiar to him and so that parents could also know their child's teacher's approach. This made it easy for the office to support the classroom teachers and quickly clarified the idea that the responsibility to *create* a positive learning environment rested primarily with the teacher, the responsibility to *support* that environment rested primarily with the office, and the responsibility *to change the behavior* rested primarily with the student—with support from the home and school.

As the year progressed at Wilson, Vice Principal Jones and the staff continued to develop their common expectations and face issues through their new lens of collective accountability. Some issues took more than a school year to resolve, and it was important not to get caught up in doing everything all at once.

Revising Procedures

One issue concerned the school's approach to dealing with late students. The traditional response was to punish the offender with detentions, which sent chronic offenders on the path to eventual removal from school. Staff members were committed to trying something new, and they recognized that there was not an adult among them who could make the claim of never being late—especially for staff meetings! The staff became more focused on how they could respond to student lateness in a more constructive way. This resulted in an agreement to implement a structured response to late students. The school would take action only after a student exceeded five unexcused tardies in a reporting period.

Initially, some feared this would lead to rampant tardiness. This fear did not materialize. (Remember the pyramid analogy and the notion that the greatest number of students will follow the rules.) The inconsistent application of the traditional response to lateness was now replaced by acknowledgment that issues occasionally arise that may keep students from being on time. Instead of immediate punishment, staff gave quiet reminders of the need to be on time and engaged students right as class started in what became a softer approach to eradicating tardiness. As a result of the change, staff members felt less stress and had to complete less paperwork and do less follow-up. They also reaffirmed the important role of modeling the correct behavior. Students had a greater awareness of the importance of being on time. When it came time to implement the new policy, however, it became evident that tardiness was a complex issue, and the new policy didn't address all its fine points, as shown by Sara's story.

> Sara showed up in tears to the office one morning. "I try to get here as quickly as I can. It's not my fault, and I don't think it's fair that I get punished," she said. She was late in the mornings quite regularly because she had three younger siblings at home and her mom was a single parent. Part of Sara's morning routine was helping get her siblings fed and to school while her mother dealt with the baby and got ready for work.

> Sara described the different reactions she got from her teachers to her tardiness. Her language arts teacher went out of her way to make Sara feel welcome whenever she arrived and praised her for her contributions to the class. Her math teacher suggested that if she was always going to be late and miss important material, she might be better off not attending at all. Needless to say, Sara redoubled her efforts on those mornings when she had language arts first and strayed a little longer when math was on the horizon.

In Sara's situation, the school should have been celebrating that she showed up at all, and yet she was facing consequences despite her effort and desire to be at school. After discussing the issues raised by Sara's story and others like hers, Vice Principal Jones and the staff made further refinements of the new policy. Staff members spoke with students identified as chronic late arrivers to explore the reasons for their tardiness. More often than not, they had a strong rationale. For those few who did not have a good reason, a program of support involving the home was the next logical step. Ultimately, the "great late debate" took on less and less importance, and staff members identified and responded to more challenging issues. As staff dealt less with these types of behaviors, they found they had more time to focus on teaching and learning.

Providing Positive Support

The staff also committed to building positive acknowledgments into their processes. They chose SMILE cards as a way to do this, and staff embarked on the process of catching students who were setting positive examples for others. (We explore strategies for positive reinforcement, such as SMILE cards, in more detail in chapter 3.) This was also an opportunity to get collective commitment from community stakeholders. Local businesses donated prizes, such as free lunches and movie passes, and the local newspaper featured photos of SMILE recipients. As a result, much more positive talk about the school began to filter through the community.

Creating a Behavior Matrix

During one of Wilson's annual reflection meetings, it became apparent that they needed to further the work they were doing to encompass common expectations for student behavior. They used a behavior matrix for this activity. The matrix described the types of behaviors they expected from students and the various settings where these behaviors occurred. Lengthy discussions and reflection by all stakeholders resulted in the identification of the school RULES:

- **R**espect self, others, and school property.
- **U**ndertake responsibility.
- **L**isten attentively.
- **E**ncourage others.
- **S**tay focused.

These rules were broad enough to encompass all expected behavior, but they could be interpreted to deal with specific misbehavior within the broad category. For example, although they did not spell out a specific rule about vandalism, a student engaged in such an activity was obviously not showing respect for the school or responsibility. They extended the activity by looking at each expectation in various settings, such as in the classroom, in the cafeteria, in hallways, and on buses, so students and other stakeholders would understand the expectations in multiple contexts.

In addition to being a tool for staff, students, and parents to use when talking about what appropriate behavior means in and around the school, the matrix also helps staff examine where particular behaviors occur in the school. The matrix is a "living document" in two important respects: it is actively used to communicate expectations to all stakeholders, and it may be revised as new challenges and opportunities to improve learning environments emerge. Some refer to the matrix as their *code-in-action*.

The behavior matrix concept originated with the work of the PBIS network (www.pbis.org) mentioned in chapter 1, and it has evolved with our own work in schools. Many schools have used the matrix as a template to modify their existing school codes of conduct. Figures 2.1, 2.2, and 2.3 (pages 30–33) show examples of elementary, middle, and high school matrices.

Khowhemun Elementary
Our Code-in-Action

😊	Be Respectful	Be Responsible	Be Safe
Classrooms	Use inside voices. Work cooperatively. Listen to others. Take turns talking. Be kind and helpful.	Try your best. Be on time. Be prepared. Follow the rules. Look after supplies.	Hands off. Use your WITS.* Listen to the teacher. Wear inside shoes. Keep clean and tidy.
Halls and entrances	Talk quietly. Be polite to others. Respect other people's things. Wait your turn.	Come in right away when the bell rings. Wipe your feet. Keep cloak-rooms neat and organized.	Walk. Keep your hands and feet to yourself. Clear hallways quickly. Always wear shoes.
Outside lunch, recess, and other times	Talk nicely. Be friendly. Listen to others. Share and take turns. Include others.	Follow rules. Play in the proper area. Take care of sports equipment. Report problems.	Play safely. Hands off. Use your WITS.* Stay in bounds. Follow the play-ground schedule.
Gym and assemblies	Listen to the teacher or main speaker. Respond politely. Be kind to those around you.	Follow gym rules. Enter only with adult permission. Take care of gym equipment.	Wear inside shoes. Keep your hands and feet to yourself. Listen to instructions. Enter and exit safely.
Eating times	Sit in your seat. Eat your own food. Whisper. Be friendly.	Listen to supervisors. Bring healthy food. Clean up your area.	Eat your own food. Clean up your food mess. Wash your hands. Stay calm and quiet.

*WITS is our peaceful problem-solving strategy: walk away, ignore, talk it out, seek adult help.

Figure 2.1: Sample of an elementary behavior matrix.

Quamichan Middle School

Respect for Self, Others, Environment, and Learning

Settings	Expectations		
All settings	Be prepared to give your best. Dress, speak, and act appropriately. Enter the school with 'uy'shqwaluwun.* Look after your school.	Keep your hands and feet to yourself. Be considerate. Use good manners and appropriate language.	Recycle. Keep the school clean. Keep the school free of vandalism and graffiti.	Be prepared with home-work and supplies. Respect others' efforts and contributions. Be a good listener.
Hallways and stairs	Walk to the right. Use inside behavior. Keep moving.	Use appropriate voice. Keep hands and feet to yourself. Be aware of space.	Help keep school clear of debris/litter. Enjoy, respect, and appreciate displays and space.	Remember to be quiet in the halls and stairwells.
Field (outside)	Respect equipment and space. Play safe. Follow expectations.	Respect personal space. Use appropriate language. Practice sportsmanship.	Place litter in the gar-bage cans. Take care with school property.	Follow instructions and rules. Use observation skills to promote safety. Be positive with classmates.

*"Uy'shqwaluwun translates loosely to "good feelings in your heart."

Figure 2.2: Sample of a middle school behavior matrix.

continued →

Settings	Expectations			
Multipurpose room and assemblies	Remain quiet and still during performances. Respect equipment. Keep your eyes on the speaker.	Clap at the appropriate time. Don't interrupt performances. Keep hands and feet to yourself. Maintain an aisle in the bleachers/on the floor.	Treat seating appropriately. Use inside behavior. Eat and drink elsewhere.	Use listening skills. Focus on the given task. Use your good manners. Follow seating instructions.
Library and computer lab	Work quietly. Explore opportunities appropriately. Respect equipment.	Wait your turn. Put things in their proper place. Follow procedures for use of equipment.	Keep area tidy. Replace the things you use. Eat and drink elsewhere.	Share materials and equipment as needed. Use appropriate research sites. Respect equipment.
Gym	Wear appropriate clothing and footwear. Moderate your voice level. Focus on the speaker (listening skills). Participate as needed.	Encourage others to do their best. Follow the rules. Share equipment. Learn/follow safety rules.	Use equipment appropriately. Keep it clean. Eat and drink elsewhere. Wear clean gym shoes.	Use your listening skills. Know and practice rules. Pay attention.
Bus	Travel safely. Sit appropriately.	Demonstrate courteous behavior. Follow driver's rules and instructions.	Care for the bus. Wait in designated areas.	Follow inside behavior rules.

Expectations	Instructional Times and Places	Noninstructional Times and Places
Respect	Let the teacher teach. Let your classmates learn. Be courteous. Treat property with care.	Be aware of the needs and concerns of others. Behave safely. Be courteous. Treat property with care.
Effort	Work through the entire class. Complete all work on time. Plan for daily activities. Keep work organized and neat.	Include others in conversations and activities. Be committed to teams, clubs, and activities. Plan for daily activities. Use garbage cans and recycle.
Attitude	Be a willing participant. Accept personal responsibility. Accept that all individuals are unique. Treat others fairly.	Be a peacemaker. Take pride in our school. Accept that all individuals are unique. Treat others fairly.
Leadership	Take initiative. Be a positive example for others. Encourage others to be involved. Encourage/practice positive risk taking.	Encourage and support others. Be a positive example for others. Include everybody. Invite participation in school clubs and activities.

Figure 2.3: Sample of a high school behavior matrix.

Covey (1989) advises us to begin with the end in mind. This is true of the behavior matrix as well. Simple schoolwide rules give students, staff, and parents a clear picture of the vision for behavior and school climate.

Often when we work with individual schools or whole districts, we ask staff to recite their school mission statement from memory. Not once has anyone been able to meet that challenge. If the principal and staff can't do it, you can be certain that students and parents can't either! Mission statements can serve a useful purpose, but common expectations—specifically common expectations that staff and students can identify and understand—are more critical than mission statements. If the expectations are easy to recall, they are also easier to follow. In every school that we have helped implement the seven keys to a positive schoolwide climate, students and staff have all been able to repeat and explain the common rules. In one school with a behavior matrix, all students and staff could explain that the common rules were to "be respectful, be responsible, and be safe." More importantly, most could give examples of what that looked like in specific areas in the school.

These common expectations are more than just rules; they create a vision of the end we have in mind. They reflect our core values in a few simple statements that everyone can remember and reference. They are more than mission statements posted on a wall to be forgotten. Everyone in the building knows them because they are repeated often within real-life contexts and modeled consistently by the adults in the school, and students understand and practice them. The behavior exemplified in the matrix becomes a habit and a way of being in the school.

Building and Implementing the Behavior Matrix

There is no single best way to build a behavior matrix in your school. There are, however, some important considerations as part of the building process.

- Staff, not administrators, should determine common schoolwide expectations through a process to reach consensus. Consensus does not always mean that there is unanimous agreement, but that "the will of the group is evident" (DuFour et al., 2010, p. 228). This can be done in various ways, all of which require that all points of view have been considered. DuFour and his colleagues recommend a strategy called "fist to five" (2010); after sharing all points of view, everyone rates their commitment to the expectations on a scale of one to five with a show of fingers. Many schools we've worked in include students in this process as well.

- The top three to five expectations identified are those the staff sees as priorities and are willing to model.

- The expectations should be positively phrased and describe observable behavior. This allows staff to use the expectations as teachable moments so students know not just what they did wrong, but what behavior is expected of them.

- Specific settings in which behaviors are expected should be relevant to the individual school.

- Descriptions of behavior should be in age-appropriate language.

- The matrix can be condensed into one user-friendly page.

The behavior matrix is only a living document or code-in-action if it is used on a regular basis by adults and students in the school. If it is not used, then it risks becoming a dust collector.

Fortunately, there are many ways—limited only by the energy and imagination of the staff—to make this tool a living document in your school. The following are some examples of ways we have seen schools make their matrix meaningful:

- One elementary principal visited each classroom in the fall, released the teacher, and used the time to do some hands-on teaching and learning with students. The topic was the code of conduct, and the lesson was built around students acting out "What does it look like and sound like to be respectful on the playground or in the halls?" In the reflection component of the lesson, students created posters to describe visually one box of the behavior matrix. By the time the class visits were complete, the principal had a large collection of student-generated posters reminding everyone of the code of conduct in action. The posters were displayed throughout the school.

- An elementary principal committed to presenting the matrix to 100 percent of the parents at her 800-student school. Through sessions offered during back-to-school night, on parent conference days, and by direct invitation, every parent received information on the matrix.

- At a middle school, homeroom teachers worked with their advisory classes on one segment of the matrix. For example, one class took on "Be safe in the gym" and another "Be responsible in the classroom." Each class worked on role-playing different scenarios to present in front of their peers. Students selected two of the class role plays to share at an assembly. Later, each homeroom took a turn re-enacting a different component of the code-in-action in front of the whole school at assembly. This was a fun way to reinforce expectations in kid-friendly terms.

- During an advisory class in a high school, a group of peer tutors met with students to discuss the behavior matrix in terms that were meaningful to the 11th- and 12th-grade students. For added emphasis, the counselor in charge of the peer-tutoring program also invited businesspeople from the community to visit the class and make the link between the behavior expectations at school and behavior expectations in the workplace. The connections were powerful.

- Many schools have sent the behavior matrix home or included it in the student agenda to help parents know and reinforce school behavior expectations at home. Other schools have included the one-page matrix document as part of a handbook for substitute teachers. These are important ways of communicating expectations to the broader school community.

Using the Matrix to Reinforce Common Expectations

All students need to learn the common behavior expectations and review them regularly. Students in the green zone can often be the best role models for those in the yellow and red zones. The bulk of our students are in the green zone, and we need to recognize their continued good behavior, thank them for it, and reinforce it in positive ways. Ideally, there should be more positive reinforcement of appropriate behavior than identification of the negatives. The matrix serves as the curriculum when students in the yellow and red zones require reteaching and reminders about the code. (We discuss positive reinforcement strategies in more detail in chapter 3.)

The behavior matrix makes the routines and life of school more meaningful. The more we use the matrix to reinforce common expectations, the more impact it will have. Schools that have had the most success at implementing and maintaining a positive learning environment over time have found ways to make the common behavioral expectations an integral part of the school day, week, and year. For example:

- A number of the schools we've worked with now have their core code phrases (for example, the RULES statements noted earlier) posted in many places for high visibility. A few examples of the places we've seen them emblazoned include over front doors, above entrances, on posters in key areas, and on letterhead. Many schools put them on tokens, such as merit points, house team points, or the SMILE cards mentioned earlier. Students can redeem these for individual, class, or team awards.

- Some schools have elected to post only the specific portions of the code that apply to a particular setting (for example, behavior in the gym), allowing for the code to be enlarged for easier reading. One elementary school posted portions related to behavior in the restroom, in each stall and above urinals and sinks.

- Some schools build key phrases into the text of their office referral forms and use them as prompts when debriefing students who have needed problem-solving time or have been given behavior consequences.

- Many schools have used the matrix expectations headings as the basis for new merit point tickets, which are given out when staff members catch kids being good. A lot of schools use the merit points as a team-building tool toward house team points; many use them for random drawings and prizes for occasional tangible reinforcement. Still others use the merit points as a concrete reminder for staff and students that the adults honor and appreciate it when students display the desired expectations.

- Some schools use matrix themes as the basis for assemblies. For example, students or staff may share examples on a theme such as *respect*. These assemblies should be age appropriate. For example, an elementary school may do student skits, while a high school may have students or guest speakers give presentations. A school Tom and Charlie worked with created its own DVD based on the *Matrix* movies and talked about behavioral expectations using this theme. They involved the entire student body in some aspect of the production, thereby ensuring buy-in from all students.

- Several school principals post the behavior matrix on the office wall at student level. At least one principal we know asks any student who is sent to the office to identify which box best describes the reason that he or she was sent in the first place. This is a powerful way to reinforce the behaviors valued by the school community. It has the added benefit of putting the ownership of the problem directly with the student in a way that focuses on the student's behavior, not his or her personality.

- Teachers, when debriefing with students who have had a problem, often use the same language contained in the behavior matrix to keep the conversation from falling into the "blame and deny" scenario we have all heard before: "I didn't do anything." "He started it." "She hates me." "It's not my fault." Instead, the conversation stays focused on the behavior expectations familiar to all involved. For example, a teacher might say, "Tawnya was not being safe in shop class as defined by the behavior matrix." This statement focuses on the behavior, not the person. This helps when communicating with parents as well, since this type of neutral message is often easier for parents to receive.

- Many teachers have woven the lessons and language from the behavior matrix into a "curriculum of caring," which we elaborate upon in chapter 3.

These and many other similar strategies have one important thing in common: they reinforce the common behavior expectations and provide a climate more conducive to productive learning. When students are given the opportunity to make personal meaning of the expectations and to understand why they are important, they are much more likely to internalize them.

Collaboratively developing a set of common expectations among all stakeholders is a critical first step. Specifying exactly what positive behaviors look like is an important component of developing common expectations. Clearly teaching, modeling, and reinforcing these behaviors for students and all other stakeholders, staff and parents included, is a critical next step. These important topics will be the focus of the next chapter.

Chapter 2 Checklist

How Do We Establish Common Expectations?

Goal	Long-Term Vision	First Steps
Achieve collective responsibility.	Staff view the success of all students as part of their professional practices.	☐ Share successes across the grade levels. ☐ Analyze case studies as a staff. ☐ Vertically collaborate. ☐ Horizontally collaborate.

continued →

Goal	Long-Term Vision	First Steps
Craft a behavior matrix.	Staff reach consensus on those behaviors that are most significant to student and school success.	☐ Review data. ☐ Collect and validate anecdotal evidence. ☐ Identify 3–5 behavioral attributes concisely and appropriately. ☐ Define age-appropriate expectations for students and staff. ☐ Identify settings (environments) across the campus for which it is most important to articulate appropriate behaviors.
State positive expectations.	Craft statements that positively state the way in which students will appropriately behave in settings across the campus.	☐ Identify behaviors that *disrupt* learning. ☐ Articulate the optimally desired behaviors that will *support* learning. ☐ Write 3–5 specific, observable behavioral characteristics for each broad behavioral attribute in each identified setting.
Model the behavioral expectations.	Staff explicitly and intentionally model the behaviors that they expect students to exhibit.	☐ Identify specific ways in which staff can model the behaviors they expect to see from students. ☐ Identify specific times and settings during which staff can model the behaviors they expect to see from students. ☐ Develop a respectful way in which staff can hold one another accountable to effectively and positively modeled behaviors.

*Visit **go.solution-tree.com/behavior** to download a copy of this chart.*

three

Targeted Instruction and Positive Reinforcement

Marzano (2003) refers to the three major roles of effective teachers as (1) making wise choices about the most effective instructional strategies to employ, (2) designing classroom curriculum to facilitate student learning, and (3) making effective use of classroom management techniques. Each of these components is critical to the creation of an effective classroom, but none in isolation will guarantee effectiveness or student learning. Marzano concludes that "a strong case can be made that effective instructional strategies and good classroom curriculum design are built on the foundation of effective classroom management" (p. 4). This chapter focuses on this foundation of effective classroom management and its relationship to student success.

In any conversation about student success, we must begin by defining success. We believe that the definition must be as broad as possible to include social, emotional, academic, and behavioral success. To create this individualized success requires a focus on targeted instruction of social skills and a commitment to positive reinforcement for each student. It involves the creation of a curriculum of caring.

Creating a Curriculum of Caring

A caring atmosphere is essential in establishing a safe learning environment in which students feel secure enough to take risks and share ideas. This is supported by the effective schools research that clearly identifies a safe, caring, and orderly environment as a critical factor in school effectiveness (Lezotte, 1997). Shelley Harwayne (1999), principal of the celebrated Manhattan New School in New York, elaborates on the importance of a caring social tone and a curriculum of caring:

> I learned a long time ago that it doesn't matter what curriculum decisions we make, what instructional strategies we try, or what assessment tools we select, if students and teachers don't care about each other. It doesn't matter how brilliant our mini-lessons are or how clever our conferences are if children make fun of each other's handwriting, dialect, or choice of topic. These things don't matter at all if the really important stuff isn't in place.

> Children will not share significant stories, take risks as spellers, or accept
> new challenges if the classroom is not secure or supportive. (p. 104)

Harwayne advocates a curriculum of caring as an effective way to create a caring social tone. The social skills required for a caring social tone need to be taught directly. Students need to see adults model these skills and behaviors, they need time to practice them in authentic situations, and they need to be shown that the curriculum of caring is both valued and celebrated. Integrating these skills into other lessons and activities helps all members of the school community build that positive social tone.

While educators need to teach these skills explicitly, it is also important for the skills to be woven into the language and events of everyday life in the school. Stand-alone lectures on respect are less effective than meaningful class discussions of the respect (or lack thereof) demonstrated by a character in a novel or by a significant historical figure in social studies. Similarly, we must model what we teach. If teachers insist that promptness and preparedness are important for students, they must be willing to model the same by being ready to teach on time. If we want kids to be respectful, we need to treat them with respect and give them opportunities to interact in meaningful and respectful ways. The curriculum of caring must be more than photocopied activity sheets—it must be infused into the way the school runs.

Targeted Social Skills Instruction

When students enter a new grade, we do not assume that they know everything there is to know about the curriculum for that grade—we structure their learning for the year around what we want them to learn. Planning and preparation should not change when we turn the topic from academics to behavior. Colvin and Sugai (1988) offer a comparison of approaches to academic and behavior problems (see table 3.1), pointing out the unfortunate differences in our approaches to correcting difficulties in academics and social behaviors.

Table 3.1: Comparison of Approaches to Academic and Behavior Problems

Frequency of Problem	Academics	Social Behavior
Infrequent	Student is trying to make correct response.	Student is NOT trying to make correct response.
	Error was accidental.	Error was deliberate.
	Provide assistance.	Provide negative consequence.
	Provide practice.	Practice not required.
	Student has learned the skill and will perform correctly in the future.	Student will make the right choice and behave in the future.

Frequency of Problem	Academics	Social Behavior
Frequent	Student has learned the wrong way.	Student refuses to cooperate.
	Student has been taught the wrong way.	Student knows what is right and has been told often.
	Diagnose the problem.	Provide more consequences.
	Identify the error or learning that was missed and reteach it.	Withdraw student from normal context.
	Adjust presentation, focus on rule, provide feedback, practice, and review.	Maintain student withdrawal from normal context.
	Student has been taught the skill and will perform correctly in the future.	Student has "learned" the lesson and will behave in the future.

You can see from this comparison that there are flaws in our approach to dealing with social behavior problems. In academic situations, we are more likely to place the responsibility on the school; in behavioral situations, we blame the family and student. In academic situations, we more often proactively diagnose; in behavioral situations, we more often react and reprimand.

We need to take the same deliberate and thoughtful approach to teaching the expected social skills as we do to teaching the expected academic skills. Teaching social skills can be time and energy consuming, but these skills are learned skills, and they can be taught. There is no ideal curriculum for social skills, but we are aware of best teaching practices that have produced success in our schools. Some basic points to consider include:

- Teach social skills like academic skills. Model behaviors, structure situations in which students can practice behaviors, and provide corrective feedback.

- Integrate social and academic skills within and across the curriculum. When reviewing instructions for an academic task, reinforce the behaviors necessary for students to respectfully and collaboratively complete the task.

- Respond proactively to infrequent errors. Recognize students for behaving well and try to anticipate when students may be at risk of misbehaving.

- Precorrect for chronic errors and with those student likely to exhibit problem behaviors. Understand the antecedents that precede misbehaviors and have plans in place to prevent them.

- Teach, encourage, and reinforce classwide positive expectations. Classrooms are communities built on relationships. Positive communities of learners built on positive relationships make goals for positive behavior easier to achieve.

- Use numerous strategies and alternatives as errors become more chronic. Work collaboratively with experts within and outside the school to develop a set of supports for students who are at risk for chronic behavior problems.

- Maximize academic success to increase social behavior success. Research acknowledges that the top contributor to problem behavior at school is academic failure. When diagnosing academic difficulties, consider behavioral causes; when diagnosing behavioral difficulties, consider academic causes.

- Actively supervise students. Adults should be present where many students congregate (such as in the schoolyard or in the halls) to supervise behavior and model positive behavior.

- Have a high ratio of positive to negative interactions. Actively reinforce and recognize when students meet expectations at four times the rate that students are corrected for misbehaviors.

- Provide specific, formative feedback that "informs learners about what they have done well and what they need to do differently" (Davies, 2007, p. 32). Develop a process through which students receive frequent, immediate feedback, particularly when they prove to be at risk for behavior problems.

It is not surprising that there is no ideal social skills curriculum since schools—like students, parents, and educators—have unique characteristics. Fortunately, these best practices can be adapted to meet the needs and strengths of individual schools and their students.

Note that while the list is specific to the teaching of behavior and social skills, it is similar to what we know makes for sound academic teaching practice, including high teacher expectations; positive and supportive classrooms; opportunity to learn; curriculum alignment, coherent content, and thoughtful discourse; scaffolding students' ideas and task involvement; and practice, application, and goal-oriented assessments (Good, 2010).

Instruction in Specific Settings

The most obvious place for social skills lessons to be taught is in individual classrooms. Chapter 4 (page 55) is dedicated to support strategies and interventions—and most commonly, we think of support and intervention happening in the classroom. However, there are many places where students and adults interact during the school day that are not in the structured confines of a single classroom.

Settings such as cafeterias, gymnasiums, and playgrounds are common spaces where social skills learning can take place. Most schools have other, more specific settings unique to the site. We've worked with staff in schools where they had heated discussions about such unique settings as "the smoke pit," "the bus loop," "the forest," "the river," and "the snow boot rack," to name a few. The intent here is not to identify all of the possible areas within the school environment—just those that might pose concern for behavioral issues.

It is essential to teach students expectations for each of the specific settings within that setting. It is much more effective, for example, to teach assembly behavior in the gym—in an assembly setting. Similarly, while students can tell you in the classroom what the soccer field rules are, it is more meaningful to demonstrate and practice them on the soccer pitch.

Several schools we know use the behavior matrix as a beginning-of-the-school-year teaching tool, taking classes to the specific settings for hands-on demonstrations of the rules. In one elementary school, the principal gets to know each class in the first month of school by taking students on this walkabout and asking them to demonstrate the appropriate behavior in the different settings. This guided tour of expectations is followed up with a writing and art activity as a reflection of the learning. The student work, in turn, becomes a tool for review later and can be put on display to reinforce the message. We've seen similar strategies used in secondary schools, with student leaders or peer tutors helping give the tours and reinforce the message. And as with academics, we must also remember to practice, review, and reinforce the message throughout the year, not just in the first days of school.

The ultimate goal is for students to become self-regulating, self-monitoring, and self-motivated citizens. While we help them along that journey, we need to be prepared to teach them specific skills and provide them with the support they need to reach the ultimate destination.

Instruction for Specific Problems

In addition to specific settings, targeted instruction needs to focus on specific problems. Often these problem issues focus on a perception of a specific set of behaviors. Bullying, harassment, defiance, and fighting are commonly named problem issues when we work with individual schools. Sometimes we get requests to work with schools to help solve one of these specific problems. While we are happy to help a school community address the concerns around bullying, for example, we always note that response to a specific problem should ideally consider the whole school system and setting.

Many programs claim to be able to solve specific problems. Some of these programs are very helpful tools. From our experience, it is much more effective to use these kinds of programs within an already established system of common expectations, targeted instruction, and positive support strategies. For example, the issue of bullying can be addressed more effectively if the whole school is clear about the language and expectations regarding bullying. Targeted instruction will be much more effective if students and adults are taught the same skill set, so that everyone knows what good behavior looks like.

These specific issues are more effectively resolved with the preventive approach of a curriculum of caring, systematically woven into a schoolwide approach of positive support strategies.

> Kerry was identified as a student with special needs. Her cognitive ability was severely limited, primarily because of fetal alcohol syndrome. She had a modified academic program and a significant life-skills component in her IEP, but she was integrated into the regular classroom almost all of the school day. Kerry's biggest challenge in the school setting was her limited ability to adjust to change in social settings. When frustrated by change or a perceived injustice, Kerry was quick to anger and often physically violent. The school-based team, led by the resource room teacher, created a very structured day plan and accompanying visual schedule to help Kerry with the many transitions that happen during a typical school day. In addition, Kerry's behavior plan was very individualized and took into account her typical triggers and attempted to minimize them.

> The individual plan, which was consistent with the schoolwide behavior plan, also included ways for Kerry to get reinforcement for small, successful demonstrations of appropriate behavior. The language within Kerry's plan was simple, consistent, and repetitive. Over time, Kerry had fewer violent outbursts and more successful days.

Positive Reinforcement of Behavior and Habits

Behavior is learned. Repeated behavior is the manifestation of habit. To form positive habits, students need to learn, practice, and repeat positive behavior; however, we do not want to leave the impression that we are so strongly behaviorist in our approach that we think students will salivate at the sound of a bell like Pavlov's dog. Skinner and other behaviorists make some valid points, but that kind of clinical thinking needs to be put into the context of human inter-relationships. Alfie Kohn (1996) was right when he said, "Behaviors occur in a context that teachers have helped to establish; therefore, teachers have to examine and consider modifying that context" (p. 16). Kohn went on to argue that schools should be about community, not compliance. We have stressed the importance of positive classroom communities, and the point is germane here: if a classroom is out of control, it makes sense that the teacher should reflect on his or her procedures, routines, and relationships instead of placing the blame directly on students.

Whether we are talking about schoolwide approaches to discipline or strategies to support individual students with behavior or academic challenges, the message is the same: we must remain positive and be proactive. It is far more effective to be proactive than reactive. Unfortunately, much of what has traditionally been done in the name of discipline in schools has been reactive. In the typical scenario, a student misbehaves, an adult staff member responds by sending the student to the office, and the principal doles out a negative consequence. Often, the same cycle repeats, with the same misbehavior, the same response, and the same consequence. Most teachers usually become frustrated with this cycle, wondering why the undesirable behavior does not stop. Many parents react by asking why the school can't handle its own problems. The administration gets frustrated that the teachers and parents aren't doing enough to help resolve these ongoing problems. Everyone points fingers. A lot of time and energy is spent putting out fires and blaming others for the problems.

This time and energy spent reacting to behavioral problems takes away from our main goal in schools, which should be students learning. Educators would rather teach than discipline. They would prefer to focus more on student learning and less on punishment and consequences. Parents would prefer to get positive messages sent home instead of negative ones. We need to change the focus of our approach to behavior issues from consequence and discipline to teaching and learning. And as with academic learning, for behavior learning, feedback is critical. To that end, we need to use positive reinforcement as part of our instruction.

Several studies support the notion that positive reinforcement is an effective tool in promoting prosocial behavior and academic skill acquisition (Cregor, 2008; Sugai & Horner, 2011). In his meta-analysis in *What Works in Schools*, Marzano (2003) identifies feedback and reinforcement as critical components in an effective classroom in regular school settings. Similarly, when working with students with special needs and behaviorally challenged students, Ernsperger (2002) advocates the effective use of both tangible reinforcement, which involves students earning items, and intangible reinforcement, which involves students earning social praise or recognition. Both authors recognize the risk of overusing reinforcement and caution teachers not to use reinforcements as bribes. Specifically, Ernsperger (2002) notes:

> Reinforcement is always contingent upon the student providing a correct response or exhibiting an appropriate behaviour. Reinforcement should never be used to entice a student into working or to reduce a problem behaviour once it has occurred. (p. 70)

We advocate the use of positive reinforcement that is appropriate to the student and the school setting. We also recommend moving from tangible to intangible, from tokens to verbal reinforcement, from frequent to infrequent reinforcement, and from regular to random reinforcement. Over time, the goal is to move to more intrinsic and less extrinsic reinforcement, when students make good decisions for the sake of the satisfaction it instills instead of the reward it brings.

In every school in which we have worked, we have seen school-based data to support the notion that reinforcement works. When we reinforce students' good decisions, they are encouraged to develop good habits; good habits contribute to consistently positive and productive learning environments.

In a meta-analysis on the effects of reinforcement, Cameron and Pierce (2006) conclude that reinforcement has documented positive effects in most cases. Occasionally the use of reinforcement has had a neutral effect, but in no case was there a documented negative effect—especially in interactions with the 5 percent of students who display behavioral problems. With these students, the use of reinforcement is a proven tool to reward prosocial behavior.

Christian had a long, well-documented history of aggressive, antisocial behavior. In his previous school, his pattern of behavior had resulted in him being on permanent half days—and even then, he was not making it to lunch more than a day or two a week because of his behavior. In class, he was very disruptive, calling out, destroying other students' property, and yelling and swearing at the teacher. On the playground, he was aggressive, argumentative, and hurtful. When sent to the office, he was at best defiant, at worst destructive. Swearing and threats of violence toward the principal and secretary were not uncommon.

This pattern of behavior was well entrenched upon Christian's arrival at his new school. But this new school had a principal and staff who were committed to the seven keys to a positive learning environment. Christian, his parents, and the principal had an entry meeting to let everyone know that Christian was getting a fresh start and went over the school's short, simple, and positive behavior matrix. Christian's teachers were prepared to welcome him upon arrival in their classrooms. The staff put in place a plan built on positive reinforcement.

Within a schoolwide framework of recognition and praise, Christian was given both tangible and intangible reinforcement when he showed improvement. For Christian, this required both extrinsic and intrinsic rewards. All staff members who worked with Christian were conscious of the need to "catch Christian being good" early and often, before he escalated into problem behavior patterns. Christian received a lot of verbal praise, gentle redirection, and, when he demonstrated appropriate behavior, merit points and tangible rewards. Gradually rewards changed from extrinsic to intrinsic, and from regular to random.

Christian demonstrated consistent, if incremental, improvements over time. The classroom teacher, in conjunction with a team of support staff, worked on an individualized plan. Gradually, his teachers spent less time on behavior management so they could actually do more academic work with Christian. This was not a quick turnaround, and it was by no means an easy task. Over the course of two years, Christian increased his ability to make it through full days in the classroom. He learned to self-regulate his aggression and to de-escalate his anger. He became able to time himself out, regain his composure, apologize for his behavior, and return successfully to the learning environment. Even on the (less frequent) days when his behavior escalated to the point of an afternoon home or suspension, Christian was able to handle this without kicking anyone or anything. He was able to walk out to his parents' car without the swearing and screaming matches with Mom and Dad. He stopped calling the principal and secretary any number of choice names. He also left school on these occasions knowing that the adults in the building cared about him and that he would be allowed to return another day with another fresh start. These were all measures of success.

Dawn Reithaug, an educator and behavior consultant, has identified nine needs of students with severe behavior challenges (1998, p. 62):

1. Structure, predictability, and consistency

2. Immediate, frequent, and specific feedback with consequences

3. Academic success

4. Responsibility and independence

5. Positive problem solving

6. Positive alternatives

7. Enhanced self-confidence

8. Positive school-to-home support systems

9. Documented positive change

Supporting the success of the most challenging individuals is no easy task. Indeed, most learners, both adults and young people, need many of these same things. The difference is that the students who present us with the most challenging behavior require all of these nine needs to be individualized in terms of both instruction and support. If we do not do our jobs in terms of instruction and support, these individuals are likely to fail. Sugai and Horner (2011) remind us that our level of intensity of response must match the level of intensity of behavior, and that our frequency of support and intervention must match the frequency of the problem behavior. At the top of the pyramid, this is individualized work. The good news is that if we have developed a solid, positive foundation with the base of the pyramid, we will have more energy and resources to work with this small, challenging group of individuals.

In addition, educators can use the following strategies for positive reinforcement.

4:1 Positives Challenge

The 4:1 positives challenge encourages the adults in the building to provide at least four positive interactions to a student for any one negative interaction they have with that student. These interactions range from small and informal to large and formal. There is no single correct way to do it, but it is critical to provide more positive than negative interactions. Positives may be verbal and they may be tangible, such as "caught being good" cards, but they should be liberally given.

The behavior matrix is a useful tool to support the 4:1 goal. Note that all of the behavior descriptions are positively phrased and that the authors have avoided the words *no* and *do not*. If the behavior matrix states, "Display good manners," then teachers will recognize students whenever they display this behavior.

These following two examples, one from high school and one from elementary school, briefly describe the effective use of the 4:1 positives challenge when linked to behavior expectations.

Danielle, a high school student, was struggling in most subjects, but especially in math. In a meeting with her parents and the assistant principal, it was concluded that most of her problems stemmed from behavior, not ability. Together, they identified the key behaviors that needed to improve, including attending class regularly and showing up for extra help at least twice a week. The teacher kept track of Danielle's attendance and offered rewards of free time at the end of class on Fridays if Danielle had a week of perfect attendance. In addition, the assistant principal held mandatory homework help on Tuesdays and Thursdays, where she provided lots of positive encouragement and cookies. Over the course of one school term, Danielle's attendance improved dramatically, her teachers noted increased participation from her in class, and her marks went up from the C− range to the C+ and B level.

Mikey was a rambunctious fifth grader who had difficulty staying in his seat and keeping his hands to himself. After a number of visits to the office, Mikey, his teacher, his mom, and the principal had a meeting to discuss a new behavior plan. This individualized plan focused on Mikey staying in his seat at seatwork time and not hitting or poking neighboring students. The teacher already gave out raffle tickets for good behavior in his class. It was agreed that Mikey would get a raffle ticket every fifteen minutes that he was not disruptive. This equated to four tickets per hour, for five hours each school day. At the end of each week, the teacher held a drawing in class. Sometimes the prizes included pencils and small toys, other times the reward was extra time on the playground at the end of the week. Despite the fact that Mikey was getting inundated with raffle tickets every time he was caught being good, Mikey was not winning the weekly draw. One day when Mikey was away, the teacher checked his desk. Amid the mess inside was a neat, tidy stack of unentered raffle tickets. The teacher asked the girl in the next desk over why Mikey wasn't putting the tickets in the raffle box. She replied, "I don't know, but he keeps pulling those out and saying, 'Look how many times I was caught being good!'"

In both cases, the focus was on easy-to-observe behaviors that matched the school and class expectations. The emphasis was on positive reinforcement of those behaviors that began as extrinsic rewards but which ultimately became more intrinsic for each student.

It is more effective to give students clear, positive examples than negative ones. Defining positive actions also gives adults structured opportunities to model those behaviors and proactive language.

SMILE Cards

SMILE is an acronym for Student Management in Initiating Leadership Excellence. In this strategy, students receive a SMILE card (a business card) with the phrase, "You are being recognized for setting a positive example for other students at _____ School." All staff members carry these cards and present them to students as they see positive behaviors being exhibited. The students may redeem them at the school store for a treat. Once a month, the staff draws two names of students to receive a free lunch and a movie pass. Local businesses love to be involved with this because of the positive nature of the project. As a result, the cost to the school is minimal. A similar idea employed in many schools is the "Gotcha" card, where staff members can present a student with a card because "I gotcha being good."

Postcards From School

For this strategy, hand out a recipe card to all students that is blank on one side and lined on the other. Ask students to draw a picture on the blank side to illustrate their thoughts or expectations about a particular area of study—for example, a lesson in science class. The teacher collects the picture and keeps them on file. At some point during the school year, the teacher sends the card to the student's home with a positive and encouraging message written on the lined side. The following are two examples:

- "I have been very impressed with the improvement Ryan has shown in his organizational skills. His last three lab reports have reflected his understanding of the scientific method. This has resulted in his being more on task during the lab component of class."

- "Alana continues to be a positive role model for other students in class. She routinely offers assistance to her peers and does so in a manner that positively reinforces the learning requirements."

Every student receives a card during the year. For some, even many years later, the postcard remains a prized possession.

Parent Advisory Council Awards

Parents play a huge role in the successful operation of schools and in reinforcing positive student behavior. One Parent Advisory Council (PAC) decided to start its own set of recognition awards, which were given out at the end of each term. These were not the traditional awards for excellence in academics (although they did have a prize drawing among all students who made the honor roll that term) but instead focused on students who showed improvement, made additional effort, or displayed a positive attitude at school. Every student came to realize that they could receive an award. The parents coordinated the assembly, presented the awards, and collected donations for the items they gave out.

Headliners

Community newspapers are always hungry for stories about kids and schools. You can provide the stories and shape how others view your school. Every day, in every school, there are success stories waiting to be told. Students and their families love to see their accomplishments featured in their local paper. For example, winners of classroom spelling bees and character awards can be featured, and the events can become community celebrations.

Names and Interests

Tom's number-one priority as a principal was to learn every student's name and something about that student. This was not easy, as the school's population grew to 730 students, but it was incredibly important in Tom's daily dealings with students. Asking about last night's soccer game, a favorite pet, a hobby, or a family member helped to break down barriers with students. This strategy makes students feel more connected to school, which increases their chances for success with behavior and academics. This is good strategy if you live in a small community, because you have many opportunities to interact with the students and their families outside of school. In larger schools, it helps students feel visible and meaningful within the school community. It helps them feel a connection to a place and a purpose so they don't get lost in the hustle and bustle of a larger building.

Effective Teaching and Learning

Instinctively, we know that good behavior management in a classroom is a prerequisite for effective teaching and learning. We do not, however, want to confuse teaching and learning styles with classroom management. Good behavior management does not necessarily mean students sitting silently in rows. In fact, much of the research on best practice in classrooms suggests otherwise. Fortunately, we have a wealth of resources to support the implementation of effective and engaging teaching and learning practices in the classroom. Whether we are talking about Lezotte's (1977) effective schools research or Marzano's research on what works in schools (2003), or the practical strategies encouraged by Bennett and Rolheiser (2001) and others, the common theme is threefold: (1) develop a meaningful curriculum; (2) create an engaging, constructivist learning environment; and (3) nurture an orderly and caring classroom to facilitate items one and two. The two keys discussed in this chapter—targeted instruction and positive reinforcement—correspond with these three themes.

In relation to problem behavior, we have learned that if it's predictable, it's preventable: we can predict that some students will require supplemental supports to succeed behaviorally. The next chapter will address how we can best prepare to provide these supports.

Chapter 3 Checklist
How Do We Target Instruction?

Goal	Long-Term Vision	First Steps
Effectively manage classrooms with well-communicated and reinforced structures, routines, and procedures.	Staff collaborate about their techniques for establishing structured, predictable learning environments.	☐ Devote time before the school year to reviewing ways in which classrooms will be managed and organized. ☐ During the first few weeks of school, check in with colleagues on the success of their efforts to establish efficient learning environments. ☐ During the first few weeks of school, check with students on their understanding of the rules and routines of a positive learning environment.
Consistently model, reinforce, and monitor.	Staff, at all times, talk the talk and walk the walk, faithfully reinforcing and tracking both positive and negative behaviors.	☐ Follow the same behavioral expectations as students and be open to friendly reminders from colleagues. ☐ Utilize the same method for reinforcing and/or recognizing positive behavior. ☐ Led by the administration, the staff understands and follows the way in which instances of both positive and negative behavior will be documented and monitored.

continued →

Goal	Long-Term Vision	First Steps
Explicitly teach schoolwide behavioral expectations.	Staff regularly and explicitly teach and reteach the behaviors that all students are expected to exhibit.	☐ The school sets aside time during which all students and staff receive explicit instruction on behavioral expectations. ☐ The school communicates the matrix and expectations to all stakeholders (parents, office staff, custodial staff) and shares the plan with the central office. ☐ The behavioral team anticipates times of the year during which behavioral expectations will need to be reviewed.

Visit **go.solution-tree.com** to download this chart.

Chapter 3 Checklist

How Do We Reinforce Positive Behavior?

Goal	Long-Term Vision	First Steps
Catch students being good.	Staff consistently and specifically reinforce at least four times as many positive behaviors as negative behaviors.	☐ Ensure focus on and recognition of behaviors, not personalities. ☐ Specifically describe the reasons why positive behaviors are receiving recognition. ☐ Agree to use the same methods to reinforce and/or to recognize positive behaviors. ☐ Formally or informally monitor individual and collective efforts to ensure we are recognizing four positive behaviors for every one negative behavior.

Goal	Long-Term Vision	First Steps
Build relationships.	Staff systemically ensure that every student has a positive connection with at least one adult on campus.	☐ School administration identifies students who are involved in any form of extracurricular activities. ☐ Study and implement strategies for building positive communities of learning within every classroom. ☐ Students in the yellow and red zones are assigned (formally or informally) mentors with whom they have established a connection and with whom they will check in regularly.
Provide schoolwide celebrations.	Formally and informally, the school regularly celebrates and recognizes positive behaviors.	☐ Consider a drawing or other systemwide method to further recognize students whose positive behavior has been recognized. ☐ Brainstorm rewards that are low cost or no cost, preferably academic in nature, that will appeal to students and will serve as an incentive. ☐ Ensure that external means of motivating students are balanced by internal means. Over time, the goal is to move to more intrinsic and less extrinsic reinforcement, when students make good decisions for the satisfaction it instills instead of the reward it brings.

*Visit **go.solution-tree.com/behavior** to download a copy of this chart.*

four

Support Strategies and Interventions

This chapter focuses on working with individual students, especially those who present us with some of the most challenging behaviors. As we've explored in previous chapters, the most effective way to support all students is within a positive learning environment that includes a framework of common expectations and responses. Without such expectations and responses, our efforts with any one individual student—especially students in the red zone—will be far less effective.

Before we can support these students, we need to identify who they are. As we mentioned in chapter 1, we need to be careful with labels within the pyramid analogy. The green zone, yellow zone, and red zone are broad generalizations of behavior, not permanent labels attached to any one individual student. The zones describe behavior, not personality. A student who may often be in the red zone with many visits to the office, for example, does not always present red-zone behavior.

We were reminded of the problem with labels as we facilitated a workshop with a group of several teams from different high schools in the same district. Each of the teams was able to identify a green zone, yellow zone, and red zone in their school population. (This is done anecdotally during workshops, but we recommend going back to your own school and using behavior or office data to do a more analytical summary.) At this particular workshop, one of the five high schools was the alternate high school for the other four schools. The regular high schools would send the students at the top of their pyramids—those with the most chronic behavior problems—to the alternate high school. What was most intriguing for us, as facilitators, was to hear the staff at the alternate high school observe that they too could identify a green zone, yellow zone, and red zone. This was a school full of students in other people's red zones, yet when these students were in this new setting, only a small percentage displayed red-zone behavior.

Students *can* move from red-zone behavior to green-zone behavior. Our role as educators is to support and facilitate that transition. The most effective way to do this is through the positive learning environment we have described in this book in which a framework of common expectations, supported with targeted instruction and positive reinforcement, is in place for all students. These should be followed by classroom strategies that optimize hands-on learning characterized by high rates of academic success and low rates of frustration. When these components are in place for all students, the school team is ready to focus more attention on individual students who need additional support. This chapter describes these supports.

Positive Interventions

We advocate an approach that ensures that the dignity of the student is always paramount. Every student, regardless of background, ability, performance, or behavior, deserves to be treated with respect. How we treat our students—the language we use, the tone of voice we project, and the behavior we model—all have an impact on student behavior. Our responses, particularly our initial responses, to student misbehavior are critical. We know that students will at times display challenging behaviors—and we usually know who will display these challenging behaviors, when they will display them, and what the behaviors will be. It is our job to respond appropriately. Whether we are working with the 80 percent in the green zone, the 15 percent in the yellow zone, or the most challenging 5 percent in the red zone, we must model the kind of behavior we expect from our students.

If we make mistakes in our handling of problem behavior and act in ways that are not in line with our core values, we have an opportunity to model meaningful apologies, positive problem solving, and restitution. Gossen (1998) notes that as a result of engaging in the process of restitution, "new behaviors are learned that can be used in other situations" (p. 3). Restitution can be viewed as a growth opportunity for all involved.

Hopefully any lapses in appropriate adult behavior are few. If we value the ability of our students to keep their cool and solve problems in peaceful ways, then we must demonstrate those qualities. Yelling, ranting, and belittling are not acceptable behaviors for students or teachers. If our students are to learn how to get along with people who have diverse backgrounds and different points of view, then we must let them see us being cooperative consensus builders and creative problem solvers.

Acting in this way lets students see that we truly believe in the expectations we promote. Our actions show them that we value the skills and behaviors that we teach. The way we treat each other creates the climate for all other efforts throughout the school. It sets the tone for the school community and is at the heart of any school improvement effort (Sergiovanni, 1992).

We have worked with a number of high school staffs that have identified attendance as a major behavior problem in their classrooms. These schools used a combination of positive intervention, both tangible and intangible, to address the problem. At one small rural high school, the principal took the tangible reward to a higher level and offered students with perfect attendance a chance to have their names entered into a raffle for a large flat-screen TV each semester. This got students' attention. Over a three-year period, this school saw improved rates of attendance and an increase in course completion and graduation rates for its students who were most at risk.

At one large inner-city high school, the staff agreed to focus on the positive in a less tangible manner. In addition to the traditional reactive consequences of detentions, office visits, and phone calls home, this staff agreed on a list of more proactive approaches, including:

- Being in class on time (teachers modeling the desired behavior)

- Greeting students warmly as they enter the room (building relationships)

- Being organized and starting class promptly with an engaging activity (no down time)

- Allowing students who arrive a little late to enter the room without fanfare or negative comment (not making them wait in the hall)

- Talking privately with students who display a pattern of problem behavior (not calling them out in class)

The staff's intent was to create a more welcoming tone in every classroom in an attempt to decrease the number of students being late or absent. Most staff took this positive challenge seriously. The principal made a point of overtly modeling this tone by visiting classes often to positively interact with students and teachers. On occasion, the principal would observe a staff member revert to the old way of doing business and had to reinforce the new positive approach, as in the following example.

> When the principal found a female student waiting to be let into a locked classroom, he quietly unlocked the teacher's door. The teacher, out of habit, stopped teaching to berate the student for being late.

> "Late again? Do you know how many classes you've missed this term? I don't know why you even bother to show up," he exclaimed.

> The principal stepped into the room after the student and responded to the teacher, "I'm sorry we interrupted your class. I was trying to let her in quietly as she really didn't want to miss your class. I'm sure she'll be happy to stay after class to get anything she missed from being late."

> Later, in a more private venue, the principal spoke one-on-one with the teacher to remind him of the commitments the staff had made to create a more positive tone.

Analyzing Student Behavior

There are many theories of human needs that attempt to explain or understand why people do the things they do. When you simplify them, just about all theories of motivation and behavior come down to this: we behave certain ways to either get something or avoid something. The details of what, how, when, where, and why we choose certain behaviors—and the specifics of what we are trying to get or avoid—are open to translation.

Most motivation theories, starting with Maslow's work, are based on meeting human needs. Maslow's hierarchy of needs (1954) begins with basic physiological needs and moves up the continuum from safety and security, through belonging and esteem, to self-actualization. Glasser (1998) and others who prescribe to control theories look at behavior as representing the need for control over aspects of personal need such as love, belonging, and power. Skinner (1948) and most behaviorists look through the lens of stimulus and response, where behavior is based on response to rewards and aversives. Rogers (1961) and other humanists submit that those nurtured in environments of positive reinforcement have the opportunity to fully actualize themselves. Covey (1989) suggests that between stimulus and response, the individual has the capacity for choice. Kohn (1996, 2005) and other constructivists believe that children behave certain ways based on meaning-making—that is, their understanding or lack of understanding of their world.

In the context of our work with students, we do not dwell on any one theory. We advocate a proven approach of practical strategies that work with kids. What matters more than theory is whether a strategy makes a difference. To make an effective, lasting difference, we need to meet students' needs.

When analyzing student misbehavior, we need to look at the problem and the underlying causes. This is not always easy or obvious. In fact, behavioral analyses are quite challenging for any educator to do alone. This work is best and most successfully accomplished collaboratively with other educators, such as within a PLC. These teams would probably involve all teachers at a grade level with whom a student interacts, and may also involve administrators and psychologists.

When analyzing student misbehavior, we need to ask two critical questions:

1. Why is *this student* behaving this way?

2. What will make a difference with *this student*?

We emphasize *this student* to keep the focus on the individual. The same kind of behavior may have many different causes for different students, and our responses need to be as unique as each individual.

Behavior Analysis Flowchart

It is important to be specific and methodical in our observation and analysis of problem behaviors, particularly as we work with the 5 percent of students who exhibit chronic behavior problems. The diagram in figure 4.1 (page 60), the behavior analysis flowchart, may help teams determine the reasons for misbehaviors and how to resolve them. Figure 4.2 (page 61) shows a completed flowchart. The method involves eight steps:

- Step 1—Define and describe the misbehavior using specific language and evidence.

- Step 2—Identify the consequence or reinforcement the student receives due to his or her misbehavior. When the student misbehaves, what typically happens? Is the student verbally chastised or removed from the environment?

- Step 3—Identify what it is that the student seems to be seeking. Most behavior results from a desire to gain attention or avoid a task. Does one of these apply?

- Step 4—Define behaviors that immediately precede the misbehavior. Is there a behavior or set of behaviors the student tends to exhibit before the undesirable behaviors?

- Step 5—Define the environments that immediately precede the misbehavior. What is the student doing or being asked to do? Where is the student? Who is the student with?

- Step 6—Define an alternative behavior that staff would accept temporarily that would satisfy the student's need. What options can be given to the student that the teacher is comfortable with?

- Step 7—Define the desired and acceptable behavior that the student will optimally display. Clearly define, for the student and teacher, what the desired behavior looks like and sounds like.

- Step 8—Define the consequence or reinforcement the student will receive for his or her appropriate behavior. What tangible positive reinforcement will be meaningful to the student when the most desired behavior is produced?

The ABCs of Behavior Assessment

Another tool to help with identifying the student needs behind a problem behavior is an ABC analysis. This tool, shown in figure 4.3 (page 62), is most often used in the area of special needs and is advocated by researchers in that field (Ernsperger, 2002; Sugai & Colvin, 2004). ABC analysis tools are helpful shorthand for school-based educators who usually have neither the time nor the expertise to engage in a full-fledged functional assessment. Please note that we do not advocate that the behavior analysis flowchart or the ABC analysis should take the place of an official functional assessment conducted by a qualified professional. These are provided as quick assessment tools used by the classroom teacher, resource teacher, or school counselor. When behavior is severe and/or frequent, a more qualified professional should do a complete functional assessment.

An ABC analysis helps us to identify a target behavior, analyze what might be causing the behavior to trigger, and determine what it is that reinforces the behavior in the mind of the student. In the language of functional assessment, it helps us determine what function the behavior serves for the student.

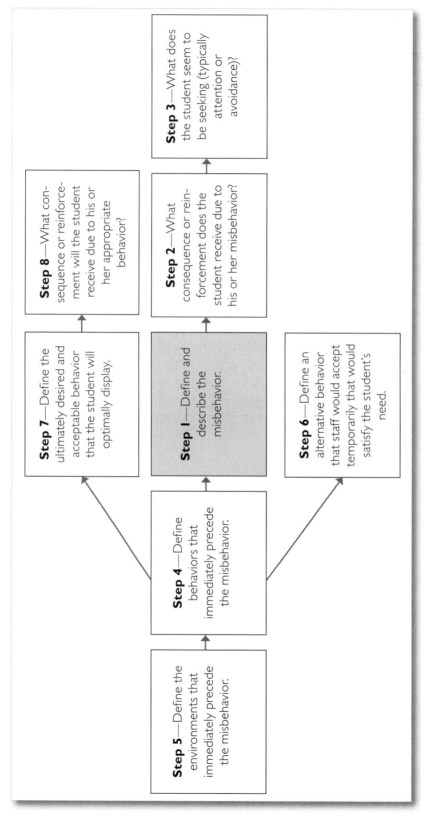

Visit *go.solution-tree.com/behavior* to download a reproducible copy of this tool, as well as a blank version.

Figure 4.1: Behavior analysis flowchart.

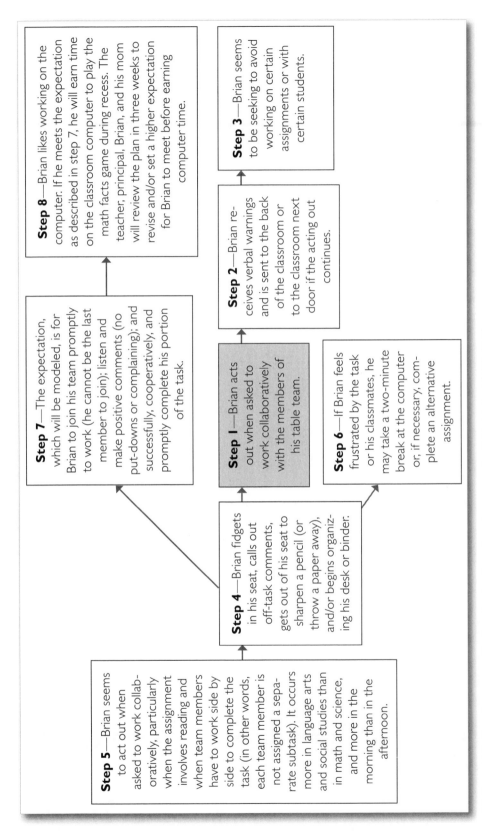

Step 1—Brian acts out when asked to work collaboratively with the members of his table team.

Step 2—Brian receives verbal warnings and is sent to the back of the classroom or to the classroom next door if the acting out continues.

Step 3—Brian seems to be seeking to avoid working on certain assignments or with certain students.

Step 4—Brian fidgets in his seat, calls out off-task comments, gets out of his seat to sharpen a pencil (or throw a paper away), and/or begins organizing his desk or binder.

Step 5—Brian seems to act out when asked to work collaboratively, particularly when the assignment involves reading and when team members have to work side by side to complete the task (in other words, each team member is not assigned a separate subtask). It occurs more in language arts and social studies than in math and science, and more in the morning than in the afternoon.

Step 6—If Brian feels frustrated by the task or his classmates, he may take a two-minute break at the computer or, if necessary, complete an alternative assignment.

Step 7—The expectation, which will be modeled, is for Brian to join his team promptly to work (he cannot be the last member to join); listen and make positive comments (no put-downs or complaining); and successfully, cooperatively, and promptly complete his portion of the task.

Step 8—Brian likes working on the computer. If he meets the expectation as described in step 7, he will earn time on the classroom computer to play the math facts game during recess. The teacher, principal, Brian, and his mom will review the plan in three weeks to revise and/or set a higher expectation for Brian to meet before earning computer time.

*Visit **go.solution-tree.com/behavior** to download a reproducible copy of this tool.*

Figure 4.2: Example of a completed behavior analysis flowchart.

| A
Antecedent | B
Behavior | C
Consequence |
|---|---|---|
| What are the antecedents (triggers) that may have caused the behavior? | What is the behavior being analyzed? | What are the consequences of the behavior for the student? |

*Visit **go.solution-tree.com/behavior** to download a reproducible copy of this tool.*

Figure 4.3: ABC analysis form.

With careful observation, an individual or team can use this tool to construct a testable hypothesis to establish the links in the student's behavior chain. First, the team determines the behavior being analyzed. It should be observable, measurable, specific, and modifiable.

Next, the team identifies the antecedents. These are the triggers that may cause the behavior. They may include environment, context, setting events, activities, actions, or prior conditions.

Consequences are the positive or negative reinforcement a student gets (or avoids) from doing the behavior in question. Once a team identifies antecedents and consequences, they will be better able to put replacement behaviors into place using alternate antecedents and modified reinforcers.

For this to be really effective, we need to think from the individual student's point of view. Consider the example in figure 4.4.

A Antecedent	B Behavior	C Consequence
What are the antecedents (triggers) that may have caused the behavior? *Julia realizes that the teacher will call on her to answer out loud, and she knows she can't answer correctly.*	What is the behavior being analyzed? *Julia pushes her books off her desk and covers her head with her hoodie.*	What are the consequences of the behavior for the student? *Julia avoids work she finds difficult. She avoids letting peers see that she can't do the work.*

Figure 4.4: Sample completed ABC analysis form.

Behavior Contracts

Monitoring student behavior and asking students to self-monitor can be a simple and effective method of improving a student's ability to meet expectations. Behavior contracts have the potential of addressing several of the keys to positive learning environments. In the sample contract in figure 4.5 (page 64), Blake and his teacher, Mr. Beyer, have identified his specific areas of need (following directions and keeping hands to himself). Blake then self-analyzes his behavior by rating on a scale of 1 to 3 for each time period during the day. Mr. Beyer also rates Blake's behavior for the same periods and using the same scale. This data can then be analyzed on a daily and weekly basis. The form facilitates communication between Blake and Mr. Beyer, as well as with the school administrator and Blake's home. Standardizing and sharing behavior contracts across the school can help staff improve student behavior and can help students take responsibility for their own behavior.

These are things I am working on: following directions and keeping my hands to myself.

This is how I did today: 3 = great!   2 = pretty good   1 = so-so

Time of Day	Following Directions		Keeping My Hands to Myself	
	Mr. Beyer	Blake	Mr. Beyer	Blake
7:45–8:30				
8:30–9:50				
First recess				
10:10–11:20				
Lunch				
12:00–12:50				
Last recess				
1:10–2:05				

Today I earned __ points.
32 points or more = reading time
20 points or less = sentences

Figure 4.5: Sample behavior contract.

Behavior and Academics

Hopefully by now we have made this point clear, but it is worth repeating: students cannot effectively learn academically until their social and emotional needs are met. Higher-level thinking cannot occur without a safe, secure learning environment. This book is not only about behavior and positive school discipline; it is about behavior *and* academics. It's difficult to separate the two.

It is rare to find a student who demonstrates behavioral challenges who has not experienced academic frustrations in the past or is not currently experiencing academic frustrations. Too often we want to respond to misbehavior with punishment. Consider that the misbehavior may be a symptom of academic frustration, and be prepared to diagnose students' academic needs as part of the solution.

Jessica was a fifth-grade student with a giant chip on her shoulder. She acted tough and cool and liked to be feared by fellow students. Jessica also disliked reading, and while she read with accuracy and moderate levels of comprehension, she read very slowly and laboriously, which served to limit the amount of independent reading she completed. Once diagnosed with difficulty in reading, Jessica received support in reading fluency. Because of this support, her reading rate increased, as did her confidence in reading. Not coincidentally, her behavior improved, largely, it seems, because she felt successful in some academic aspect of school.

Creating Acceptable Alternatives

The more challenging step comes after the behavior analysis. Once the team has developed a testable hypothesis that appears to be accurate in predicting the triggers, behaviors, and consequences for an individual student, members need to take action: creating an individualized plan to help teach the student replacement behaviors with reinforcement that is powerful enough to extinguish the old, unacceptable behavior. The challenge is being willing to work toward an acceptable alternative—even if it is not the ideal alternative. The range of alternatives will be as unique and varied as the individual students presenting the problem behaviors. We share many ideas in stories throughout this book. Additional acceptable alternatives may include:

- Adjusting time, amount, and pace of material
- Providing alternate work spaces, settings, graphic organizers, and adaptive tools
- Allowing students to work while listening to music, chewing gum, with a partner, and so on
- Being cognizant of learning styles and strengths, and offering students choice in the way they share their learning: visual, oral, electronic, one on one, and so on
- Being open to new ways of letting students show what they know
- Building in breaks for students who can't sit still for extended periods of time that can be earned with the demonstration of the acceptable alternative behavior (may or may not include tokens and rewards)

Ultimately, we want all students to behave well all of the time—to always work to the best of their ability, never disrupt the learning of others, and behave in this manner without the need for external reinforcers. This is a lofty goal for the 5 percent of students who display chronic behavior challenges. For them, the goal is a long-term one that begins with small steps and is built on small successes, sometimes to a standard that is different from that of other students, at least over the short term. As we teach replacement behaviors and see success, we can build what Ernsperger (2002) refers to as *behavioral momentum*. Over time, and with one small success after another, we may see the student become able to meet the overall standard. This may or may not be a reasonable expectation depending on the student's other needs and challenges.

Some educators with whom we have worked have difficulty with this concept. They see it as unfair that there might be different behavior goals for some students. They complain that these alternatives take up too much time or distract too much from classroom teaching and learning. Our response is usually this: in your current situation, with a student who is exhibiting chronic volatile behavior, how much time are you losing, and how much teaching and learning is being disrupted? To obtain different outcomes, we must have the courage and willingness to try different approaches, and we must believe the research. There is a significant body of research that supports the efficacy of individualized supports for students most at risk and little or no research that supports the efficacy of one-size-fits-all approaches to academic or behavioral challenges.

Zack, a ninth-grade student, gained a reputation in his junior high school with behavior that other students called the "Zack attack": Zack running out of his class, slamming the door, and rattling the locks on lockers as he ran down the hall yelling and swearing at his teacher. These episodes usually ended with Zack climbing a tree in front of the school with the teacher and principal chasing after him and trying to get him down. A school-based team met to discuss these outbursts and analyze Zack's behavior. Using the ABC analysis, it was clear that Zack usually became most agitated before students were asked to work out a math problem on the board at the front of the room. If Zack felt that he did not have the right answer, he would get upset and misbehave at his desk. If this avoidance technique didn't work, and the teacher still called on Zack to take his turn at the front board, Zack would throw his supplies off his desk and storm out of the class. This in-class outburst was followed by the very public Zack attack. The consequence for Zack was that he avoided doing the math on the board, got lots of peer attention, and got to climb a tree.

The team decided to try something different. Before asking Zack to solve a math problem on the board, the teacher would check to see that Zack had a question he knew he could do. Whenever there was a question Zack could answer, he was invited to share that correct answer with the class. The arrangement made between the teacher and Zack was that if he could work in class without an outburst, he could earn points each day. At the end of each week, if Zack earned enough points, he and a teacher assistant could leave class ten minutes early to climb a tree. This worked. Zack was better able to cope in class, completed more math questions with fewer outbursts, and earned some free time to climb trees most weeks. The openness to these acceptable alternatives resulted in fewer disruptions for the teacher and the rest of the class. It also increased Zack's academic success while decreasing the frequency and intensity of his misbehavior.

Consistent Responses, Interventions, and Consequences

In addition to the proactive approach of common schoolwide expectations and a behavior matrix to support the teaching of these expectations, it is important for the whole school community to be clear and consistent in the response to misbehavior. There is no single best way to respond to misbehavior. What is known to be best practice, however, is that a balance of positive feedback and reinforcement combined with fair, consistent consequences is very effective. In his meta-analysis on school and classroom behavior management, Marzano (2003) found:

> Decades of research provide clear guidance on critical aspects of effective management and the strategies that work best to achieve it. Equipped with this knowledge and understanding, schools and classroom teachers can educate students in a safe, orderly and respectful environment that maximizes the possibility for effective teaching and real learning. (p. 115)

One key aspect of effective management and improved behaviors is the consistent application of commonly understood responses to inappropriate behavior. All fall within the system of common schoolwide expectations advocated throughout this book. Young people need to know the expectations, how to demonstrate them, and what the response will be when they do not adhere to them. Research supports the notion that students need a healthy balance of positive reinforcement and consistent consequences (Marzano, 2003).

Consequence is not synonymous with punishment. Students do not need to feel hurt to feel that they have learned from their mistakes. Instead of punishment, we prefer interventions and fair consequences. This is consistent with the description of discipline versus punishment described in table 4.1 and with Coloroso's (2001) notion of the "backbone" versus the "brick wall" school.

Table 4.1: Punishment Versus Discipline

Discipline	Punishment
• Is student focused • Shows students what they have done wrong • Clarifies ownership of the problem • Facilitates problem solving • Seeks resolution and leaves dignity intact	• Is adult oriented • Requires judgment • Imposes power • Arouses anger and resentment • Invites more conflict

The difference is that punishment is intended to control behavior, whereas interventions and consequences are designed to help students learn alternate behaviors. Interventions and consequences are best delivered within the framework of consistent schoolwide expectations.

The Backbone School

Coloroso (2001) describes three kinds of families: jellyfish, brick wall, and backbone. The jellyfish family, according to Coloroso, is one that lacks in structure, consistency, and safe boundaries. Children are given few limits and never learn to have inner self-discipline. A brick wall family, on the other hand, is one of strict order, control, and power. Children learn to be fearful and subservient, never having an opportunity to develop a sense of self or self-control. In the middle is the backbone family, which is typified by respect, empathy, consistency, and fairness. Children in a backbone family learn self-respect and compassion and are better able to develop a sense of empowerment and responsibility.

Based on Coloroso's definition of a backbone family, we believe a backbone school is exemplified by the following qualities:

- A network of support for students
- Democracy learned through experience
- An environment conducive to creative, constructive, and responsible activity
- Rules that are simply and clearly stated
- Consequences that are natural or reasonable, not punitive
- Discipline that includes a learning component
- Positive feedback and second chances for students
- Modeling of and encouragement for competent, cooperative behavior
- The development of self-awareness and self-responsibility in students
- Students who think for themselves

When It's Not Working, Ask Why

Let's assume you have developed a clearly articulated code of conduct; written behavior expectations in positive, student-friendly language and taught these directly to students; implemented clear steps in a support and consequence continuum; and your whole school is working on a positive learning environment. Is your school now perfect? Do kids behave exactly as expected? Do they do the right thing, even when no one is looking? Is the entire school day free from disruption, defiance, and discipline issues? We doubt it!

No school is perfect. There is nothing wrong with not being perfect. There is, however, something wrong with ignoring or denying problems. When things are not working, we need to admit it and ask why they're not working. We need to be systematic in our analysis of the problems. We must be sure to find the source, not continue to dwell on the symptom. We have to be able to respond to the problem in a way that seeks solutions, not simply to lay blame.

The good and challenging work of determining common expectations, targeting instruction, positively reinforcing appropriate behavior, and supporting students who are at risk will fade if students are not supported by collaborative teams that gather and respond to relevant data. Teams and data will be the focus of the next chapter.

Chapter 4 Checklist
How Do We Support and Intervene?

Goal	Long-Term Vision	First Steps
Establish respectful, predictable environments.	Staff acknowledge that the climates within the classrooms and across campus play a significant role in helping students make good choices.	☐ All staff commit to modeling appropriate behaviors, including adults' responses to students' poor decisions. ☐ Staff study and implement a curriculum of caring. ☐ All adults on campus acknowledge that their actions contribute significantly to student behaviors and are willing to examine changes they can make to improve challenging situations.
Diagnose antecedents to poor behavior.	Staff analyze student difficulties that lead to poor choices and behaviors so that they can address causes and not symptoms.	☐ First, staff ensure that they respectfully correct behaviors, focusing on the behavior, not the person. ☐ Staff consider that academic frustration or failure may contribute to misbehavior and attempt to specify and ameliorate the difficulty. ☐ Staff use a functional approach to determining why and what precedes poor behavior so that alternatives and precorrections can be introduced.

continued →

Goal	Long-Term Vision	First Steps
Exhibit a willingness to individualize settings and strategies for students at risk.	Staff approach the needs of students with the greatest behavioral challenges with respect, openness to alternatives, and the expectation that behavior will improve.	☐ Staff work on supporting students based in part on the nine needs of students with severe behavior challenges. ☐ Staff work collaboratively to integrate supports for students most at risk to ensure consistency. ☐ Staff recognizes that individual plans may be necessary for students with the most severe and unique needs—they may not be treated the same as others, at least temporarily.

Visit **go.solution-tree.com/behavior** to download this chart.

five

Collaborative Teams and Data-Driven Dialogue

Changing behavior from negative to positive is about results, not intentions. As DuFour, DuFour, Eaker, and Many (2006) note, "No school or district creates a results orientation by accident" (p. 119). To make the deliberate shift from intentions to results, educational leaders must create the conditions that foster collaborative relationships among teams of teachers. According to Fullan (2003), it is impossible to have long-term gains in student achievement without a high degree of trust among staff members. Fullan maintains (2003), "Leaders must establish a climate of relationship trust within which tough issues are tackled" (p. 63). Through these collaborative teams and relationships, educators create the data-driven dialogues necessary to achieve the desired results among the school community and individual students. As Glaze and Mattingly (2008) note, in a PBIS environment, "Working collaboratively with other school staff, administrators can create environments that sustain positive behavior support" (p. 55).

This chapter describes a series of actions and structures that have proven successful at both the elementary and secondary school levels in fostering collaborative relationships among staff to achieve specific desired results in both student behavior and academics.

The actions and structures described in this chapter have been successfully field-tested with many staffs and students across North America through our work with schools. In addition, one author of this book, Charlie, has been the principal at two of the featured schools. Both of these schools have diverse student populations ranging from the most affluent to the most vulnerable. A large portion of each school population is described as being from the inner city and as socioeconomically challenged. Both schools offer free breakfast and subsidized lunch to significant numbers of students (between 30 percent and 60 percent). Both schools are ethnically diverse, with particularly large percentages of Aboriginal students (between 35 percent and 65 percent). In both cases, the schools faced a troubling trend of poor academic results.

One school, Khowhemun Elementary, turned this trend around in a five-year period with exciting results. Student achievement improved. In reading, the percentages of students reading at grade level increased from 67 percent to more than 80 percent. In math, the gains rose from 65 percent to close to 90 percent. Aboriginal student results also improved considerably.

At Quamichan Middle School, staff members have seen similar improvements over a three-year period. Office referrals for problem behavior decreased from more than 2,000 per year to less than 1,200 per year, including a significant decrease in suspensions for serious offenses. At the same time, academic results increased. Scores for students reading proficiently at grade level increased from 43 percent to 69 percent over the same three years.

Relationships *and* Results

We must begin with a brief discussion of professional learning communities. In PLCs, collaborative teams use data on student behavior to implement interventions, monitor progress, and celebrate successes. While it is not necessary for schools to function as PLCs to implement the seven keys to a positive learning environment, it will certainly make the process easier. PLCs have certain structures in place that help facilitate the process of collaboration and results-based inquiry (DuFour et al., 2008):

- Shared mission, vision, values, and goals that are all focused on student learning
- A collaborative culture with a focus on learning
- Collective inquiry into best practice and current reality
- An action orientation
- A commitment to continuous improvement
- A results orientation

To create an effective PLC, a principal must build relationships *and* get results. It is not an either/or proposition. Too often, principals think that they have to either embrace the "soft" issues of collaboration and relationships *or* attack the "hard" topics of assessment and results. Collins and Porras (1997) describe this as succumbing to the ineffective "Tyranny of Or." High-performing organizations, on the other hand, strive for what they call the "Genius of And" by finding a way to do two seemingly contradictory things at the same time (pp. 44–45).

Implementing behavior interventions and creating a positive learning environment requires both relationships *and* results. It requires the critical task of collaborative teams engaging in meaningful dialogue about data. Specific actions by leaders to support collaborative inquiry include:

- Establishing a climate of trust to foster powerful collaboration
- Structuring results-based inquiry and staff development

- Developing an action orientation for implementing, monitoring, and celebrating successful interventions

Building a Climate of Trust

So how does a school staff engage in, and stay committed to, conversations focused on student success? How do they establish a climate of trust to foster powerful collaboration? DuFour et al. (2006) define collaboration in a PLC as follows:

> A *systematic process* in which educators work together interdependently to analyze and to *impact their professional practice* in order to achieve better results for their students, their team, and their school. (p. 98)

As anyone who has worked on a school staff where the focus was not on improving practice for better results will attest, simply placing teachers into teams will not guarantee that they will collaborate. A staff can begin to build a climate of trust by engaging in some form of appreciative inquiry.

Start Small

Teams should look for safe, low-risk ways to begin collaborative conversations before getting into the more sensitive conversations about hard data and results. Tools that allow staff members to self-reflect on successes and challenges provide a good starting point. For example, the OSEP Center on Positive Behavioral Interventions & Supports (www.pbis.org) provides surveys that help staff to analyze what is working well and what areas need attention in terms of behavior and discipline in their schools. *Learning by Doing* (DuFour et al., 2010) provides several self-assessment rubrics for teacher teams to use to analyze where they are on the PLC continuum. (See www.allthingsplc.info for copies of these tools.) Whatever the tool, the purpose is to provide staff an opportunity to self-reflect on successes and challenges and then work in collaborative teams to share their findings and opinions.

Tackle the Tough Conversations

As teams begin to tackle tougher conversations, such as broad changes in instructional practices that will result in more engaged and better behaved students, effective teams are sure to operate within agreed-upon team norms, which create a sense of order and safety. DuFour et al. (2006) warn that as teachers "work collaboratively to clarify the essential learning . . . and analyze the results, they must overcome the fear that they may be exposed to their colleagues and principals as ineffective" (p. 102). DuFour et al. (2010) go on to offer detailed suggestions for collaborative teams as they begin their work together:

- Each team should create its own norms.
- Norms should be stated as commitments to act in certain ways, rather than as beliefs.
- Norms should be reviewed regularly and their effectiveness evaluated.

- Violations of team norms must be addressed.

Creating and honoring team norms enhances collaboration. Here are two suggested norms for teams:

1. We'll avoid blaming—ourselves, our students, our administrators, or our families.

2. We'll focus on what *we* can do to positively impact the challenges that we face.

Collaboration does not happen by invitation. School teams need time, structures, and support to make the collaboration significant. Meaningful conversations, occurring consistently over time, supported with resources and follow-up action are what build a climate of trust within a team. DuFour et al. (2010) are emphatic on this point:

> The pertinent question is not "Are they collaborating?" but rather, "What are they collaborating about?" . . . The purpose of collaboration—to help more students achieve at higher levels—can only be accomplished if the professionals engaged in collaboration are *focused on the right work.* (p. 119, emphasis ours)

In a PLC setting, the *right work* should focus on four critical questions (DuFour et al., 2010):

1. What is it we want our students to learn?

2. How will we know if each student has learned it?

3. How will we respond when some students do not learn it?

4. How will we extend and enrich the learning for those students who have demonstrated proficiency?

Similarly, in a PBIS setting, the same four questions could be rephrased as:

1. How is it we want our students to behave?

2. How will we know if each student has learned how to behave?

3. How will we respond when some students do not behave?

4. How will we extend and enrich the learning for those students who have demonstrated proficiency?

We will return to the answering of these questions later in this chapter.

Team Specifics

Teams can be built in a number of configurations depending on the size and structure of the school. Often these will be grade or subject teams with obvious curriculum in common. This structure makes most sense when the goals are academic. Other times, teams may be multidisciplinary with other things in common. This is most often the case when it comes to schoolwide goals around behavior expectations. In schools or grades that departmentalize, the algebra or math team might collaborate weekly to discuss key math content, data, and students in need. In addition, ninth-grade teachers from math, social studies, science, English, physical education, and the arts may collaborate weekly to discuss behavior expectations and students in need of additional social and behavioral support.

Teams must meet in a regularly scheduled and structured way. DuFour et al. (2006) insist that it is "imperative that teachers be provided with time to meet during their contractual day" (p. 95). It is much less effective to do this work as an optional add-on to the day. In schools and districts where we have worked, staff have been provided with meeting time within the regular school day. This often takes the form of a structured agenda at the regular staff meeting, during early dismissal or late-start days, or in place of other mandated meetings such as student support team or school-based team meetings. Different schools and districts create this meeting time in ways that are unique to each locale.

We recommend creating distinct teams and meetings for academic goals and behavior goals. This helps maintain team focus and avoids the breakdown that can occur in meetings when people just want to complain about "the way kids behave these days." Team meetings that are clearly focused on specific goals increase the likelihood of productivity. When the teams meet is not nearly as important as what they meet about.

Results-Based Inquiry

Teams should begin their results-based inquiry by returning to the critical questions: What is it we want students to learn? Or, how is it we want students to behave? Before digging into the data to discuss results, teams must be clear on what it is they expect students to know and/or be able to show.

When discussing common expectations for behavior, teams should refer to their behavior matrix (as described in chapter 2) so everyone is clear about the expectations. The behavior matrix forms the foundation for intervention. Only after the behavior expectations are clear will teams be ready to analyze the data and be able to engage in results-based inquiry.

Universal Screening

A common question we hear from staffs ready to engage in developing a system of behavioral supports is regarding data and, more specifically, universal screening. Within an academic system of response to intervention (RTI), universal screenings are simply tools that apply (or are administered) to all students. They provide information about which students may be candidates for supplemental assistance *and* about areas of the curriculum that may require increased attention from staff due to the relative underperformance of students. For academics, these screening tools often take the form of standardized assessments (for example, the Northwest Evaluation Association's [NWEA] Measures of Academic Progress [MAP] assessments or curriculum-based measures [CBMs] such as Dynamic Indicators of Basic Early

Literacy Skills [DIBELS], which are typically administered three times a year.) There are similar tools to assist collaborative teams when responding to behavior issues.

The Student Risk Screening Scale (SRSS; see figure 5.1), is a no cost, widely available, validated tool for identifying students at risk for misbehavior (Drummond, 1993; Lane, Kalberg, Lambert, Crnobori, & Bruhn, 2009). With this assessment, teachers rate students in their classes using a Likert-type scale on seven items. The SRSS rates student risk from low (0 to 3) to moderate (4 to 8) to high (9 to 21).

The collaborative conversations that ensue from this tool are powerful and can include dialogue around the following questions:

- Which students were rated as most at risk?
- Do students identified by the SRSS match our more anecdotal, more informal (but still valid) opinions of students at risk behaviorally?
- Are there consistencies from teacher to teacher, grade level to grade level, and course to course in regard to the students rated highest?
- Which of the seven areas was rated highest within classrooms?
- How can we best respond and support students rated as at risk?
- How can we best address areas rated highest?

The SRSS can help staff members come to consensus on behavioral goals, areas on which to focus, and expectations.

Teachers at Bridges School use the SRSS as a valid and useful tool to support the school's efforts at creating more positive learning environments. Teachers at Bridges complete the SRSS three times a year for each student in their class, using the totals to screen for students who may be at risk. Classes generally have between two and six students identified as at risk. The principal initiates conversations with teachers to ask if more support could be provided. Students with more than nine total points are considered for placement into social skills groups that meet during recess, lunch, and other breaks. Even if a student is not considered for a group, he or she is screened by the SRSS again later in the year, along with the students identified as at risk, to monitor progress.

Anyone who works in education will agree there are usually far too many goals than what teachers can adequately address. As a solution to this problem, Marzano and Haystead (2008) recommended that teachers "delete content that is not considered essential, delete content that is not amenable to classroom assessment, and combine content that is highly related" (pp. 12–13). One of the most powerful ways that we have found for teacher teams to do the recommended streamlining is

Teacher Name:

0 = Never, 1 = Occasionally, 2 = Sometimes, 3 = Frequently

Use the above scale to rate each item for each student.

Student	Steals	Lies, Cheats, Sneaks	Exhibits Behavior Problem	Experiences Peer Rejection	Has Low Academic Achievement	Exhibits a Negative Attitude	Exhibits Aggressive Behavior	Total

Source: Adapted from Drummond, 1993.

Figure 5:1: The Student Risk Screening Scale (SRSS)

to collaborate on what we refer to as *priority learning outcomes*. Teams collaborate to create a set of clearly defined learning outcomes that the teachers agree are the most critical for the given grade and subject. Ainsworth (2003) referred to these as *power standards*. Teachers appreciate this time and focus, as one individual with whom we worked noted:

> At the school where I have worked for almost ten years, we have spent a significant amount of time (and money) to work together in subject-area teams to create "priority learning outcomes." When I speak to other schools about these priority learning outcomes, they are baffled that our administrator would agree to, organize, and support this for us.

Once the team is clear on what it is they are expected to teach, they can then work on how it is they are going to assess their students' progress.

The behavior matrix creates a clearly articulated set of expectations for behavior, and the SRSS can validate staff decisions about which students may need additional support and broaden or deepen conversations and understandings of behavior expectations and student needs. We recommend that academic teams create an assessment matrix for each of their priority learning outcomes. These are more commonly referred to as *assessment rubrics*. Once teams become comfortable working together to create these priority learning outcomes, we encourage teams to take this work another step further and write them in student-friendly *learning intentions* so that students are also clear on the expectations for learning. Doing this work together also builds staff capacity. According to Glaze and Mattingly (2008), "Having all staff participate in developing the plan increases ownership and support for implementing and maintaining it" (p. 58).

Developing an Action Orientation

When teacher teams are able to engage in these conversations to the degree that they can identify students requiring intervention and take action based on the data, this change represents a profound cultural shift—a shift in focus from teaching to learning and from intentions to results. DuFour et al. (2008) identify this cultural shift as necessary in schools that seek to function as PLCs. In chapter 4, we described structures for support strategies and intervention. Here we describe how the presence of collaborative teams enhances those structures.

Teams that become comfortable with sharing data and analyzing results tend to take the data personally. In the data, they see the names of individual students, not just the statistics. They take action based on the results. In fact, DuFour et al. (2006) remind us that PLCs address the ultimate issue: "How can we use this evidence of student learning to respond to our students and to improve our individual and collective teaching?" (p. 189).

When analyzing data, it is helpful to have structures to keep team meetings focused. We recommend an agenda and a record-keeper at the very least. Team members need to share the responsibility of bringing classroom data to share, providing copies of assignments and assessments, sharing strategies that have worked, and suggesting interventions that might be helpful for individual students. Team leaders, with the support of the principal, should collate the data and help make it meaningful and important to the team. One team leader with whom we worked observed the following:

> One way in which the principal has done this has been through building his team leaders right into the school plan. For example, he noticed that his team leaders had independently taken an interest in both instructionally intelligent teaching strategies and assessment for learning strategies. Rather than being the resident expert in these areas, he encouraged other teachers to approach team leaders for ideas or support. He leveraged these strengths in his team leaders by writing them and their areas of strength right into the school plan. Presently, there are four strategies in the school plan for improved literacy skills in all curricular areas; similarly, there are four team leaders, each of whom is responsible for promoting and supporting their area of strength or interest. These types of structures will assist teams in the setting and monitoring of goals.

Setting SMART Goals

We will discuss goal setting and monitoring more fully in chapter 6, A Schoolwide Systems Approach, but it is important to make the connection between collaborative teams, data-driven dialogue, and SMART goals here. Collaborative teams working within a climate of trust where team members are comfortable sharing results routinely develop and analyze SMART goals, or goals that are:

- Strategic and specific
- Measurable
- Attainable
- Results-oriented
- Time bound

We have worked with school teams that have effectively used the SMART goals process for both behavior and academic goals. The process is the same.

The process of setting data-driven goals and reaching them encourages leaders to "break down big problems into small, doable steps . . . plan for small wins. Small wins form the basis for a consistent pattern of winning that appeals to people's desire to belong to a successful venture" (Kouzes & Posner, 1987, p. 218). Patterson et al. (2008) advise that "it's best to take complex tasks and turn them into small, achievable goals. . . . Don't wait until people achieve phenomenal results, but reward small improvements" all along the way (p. 205). Both Fullan, Crevola, and Hill (2006) and Schmoker (1999) support this process with their notion of breakthrough strategies focused on small but immediate improvements toward larger goals.

Mining the Data

How do we know if we have met our SMART goals? We must gather the data from formative and summative assessments (assessments *of* learning and assessments *for* learning) and progress-monitoring probes to inform and evaluate our systems of support and to determine if students are responding to our instruction and intervention. How might this look in the behavioral realm? How will we know whether we have small improvements to celebrate and reward? It means accumulating more data on behaviors than we currently gather, and rethinking the traditional behavioral referral.

Referrals have traditionally been completed for students committing major violations of school rules. Data from referrals for major violations of behavioral expectations (or for violations of a serious nature) will not sufficiently inform our monitoring and adjustment of student behaviors, nor will they provide a sufficient amount of data for us to evaluate the efficacy of our efforts. Schools may need to rethink the traditional referral and adopt what we call a *behavior documentation form* (see figure 5.2; also, the OSEP Center on Positive Behavioral Interventions & Supports [www.pbis.org] provides numerous excellent examples of school referral forms). These behavior documentation forms, or BDFs, are an efficient way for staff to manage referrals, particularly when using databases such as the School-Wide Information System (a web-based information system designed to help school personnel use office referral data to design schoolwide and individual student interventions).

With data from these BDFs, teams focusing on behavior issues would be in a position to answer the following critical questions:

- Which students are experiencing difficulties?
- Are students to whom we have provided more intensive, individualized supports responding?
- Which teachers, classes, or grade levels may need additional supports?
- With what types of behaviors are students experiencing difficulties?
- In what settings across campus are students experiencing difficulties?

The BDF can also serve as a communication tool between families and schools, between the office and teachers, and between staff and students. When teams and teachers analyze a student's behaviors in an attempt to determine possible antecedents to and explanations for misbehavior, the "others involved" and "motivation" fields can provide important information.

The process of gathering data and generating information from the BDF should be efficient since staff can mark fields within the BDF and databases such as SWIS allow for easy data entry and data analysis, allowing staffs to analyze, monitor, and adjust their practices based on real-time data. In our experience, it takes time to establish the BDF process in a school. Schools must be comfortable processing many more BDFs per day than in the past. (In our experiences, schools of 500 students would generate approximately fifteen BDFs per day, which require approximately

School Behavior Documentation Form (BDF)

Student name: _____

Date: _____   Time: _____   Staff: _____

Location:
_____ classroom   _____ walkway   _____ library   _____ restroom   _____ playground   _____ lunch area

Major:
_____ abusive/inappropriate language
_____ fighting/physical aggression
_____ defiance/disrespect/ noncompliance
_____ lying/cheating
_____ harassment/bullying
_____ disruption
_____ truancy
_____ property damage
_____ forgery/theft
_____ use/possession of controlled substance/weapon

Minor:
_____ inappropriate language
_____ physical contact
_____ defiance/disrespect/noncompliance
_____ disruption

Follow-up action(s):
_____ no recess (_____ recess/days)
_____ conference with student
_____ parent contact
_____ privilege loss
_____ (_____)
_____ time in office
_____ in-house suspension
_____ out of school suspension (_____ days)
_____ other:

Comments:

Others involved: _____ none   _____ staff   _____ teacher
_____ unknown   _____ peers (_____)

Motivation: _____ obtain peer attention   _____ avoid task/activity
_____ don't know   _____ avoid peer   _____ obtain adult attention
_____ avoid adult   _____ obtain item/activity

Parent signature. Return to classroom teacher.
Parent signature: _____
White = office
Yellow = parent
Pink = teacher

Figure 5.2: Sample behavior documentation form.

ten minutes of office time to enter into a database.) Some staff members used the BDFs too often, and others not enough. Staffs should discuss how many accumulated minor infractions would lead to a major infraction, how to best collect BDFs, who is responsible for contacting parents and under what circumstances, and so on. In our experience, BDFs are extremely effective monitoring and teaching tools—they provide a document that facilitates corrective conversations between staff and students. Administrators and teachers can refer to the BDFs when reviewing behavioral infractions with individual students because all relevant data is included.

Maintaining a Sharp Focus

Before concluding this chapter, let's acknowledge that we currently face a dilemma in education, whether perceived or real. We feel as though we are working as hard as we can, and yet we're being asked to ensure that students—*all* students—achieve at higher and higher levels. Let's assume that we are working as hard as we can, and let's assume that we truly want to help *all* students achieve at higher and higher levels and that we even celebrate and embrace this responsibility. What do we do?

First, we must work collaboratively. One of the most intelligent ways to perform our work is to share ideas, share the load, and share successes. The only way we'll accomplish our increasingly lofty goals is by systematically and faithfully working together. Building a system of behavioral supports will require the participation of all staff in collaborative teams as much as any endeavor to which a school commits.

Next, we must focus our work because, as the saying goes, when everything is important, nothing is important. Collins (2001), in his study of great organizations, concluded that focus is essential. He makes the case that a focus on a few carefully selected goals, combined with an intense focus on ensuring the success of our efforts in pursuit of these goals, will lead to improved performance. We must have the courage to find a focus and remain focused. Start small, engineer early victories, and build momentum. Building a system of behavioral supports is important, high-leverage work. If it's not one of the top two or three areas of focus for your school and your collaborative teams for a period of several years, and if you have not defined your goals and expectations as described here, then you're not focused.

The final chapter of this book, A Schoolwide Systems Approach, describes how the first six key components for a positive learning environment can be integrated into an efficient and effective schoolwide system. Chapter 6 gives practical examples of how schools and school leaders can lead and manage the critical components of the system of behavioral supports to maintain momentum and ensure success.

Chapter 5 Checklist

How Do We Create and Sustain Collaborative Teams?

Goal	Long-Term Vision	First Steps
Establish and adhere to team norms.	Staff respectfully and cooperatively collaborates on the topic of students and student learning with a spirit of trust, professionalism, and compromise.	☐ Agree upon norms that will guide conversations and work. ☐ Provide at least one hour per week of time during which collaboration about students and student learning takes place. ☐ Focus on the four critical questions of PLCs as a key norm for teams.
Teams focus on what they can do and measure their results with evidence.	Staff respects and appreciates the external realities that affect their work but continuously focus on positive actions they can take and on the results of these actions.	☐ Do not become distracted or discouraged by the factors that complicate and challenge the work to be completed. ☐ Focus on purposeful actions that can be taken. ☐ Do not judge success based on implementation—judge success based on evidence of student growth.
Teams share knowledge and workload.	Staff share successes and challenges in a climate of trust and meaningfully contribute to the shared work of the team.	☐ Share the best, most effective strategies. ☐ Be open to implementing new strategies. ☐ Accept responsibility and complete tasks for the team. ☐ Deconstruct goals, identify specific tasks, and assign tasks to team members.

*Visit **go.solution-tree.com/behavior** to download a copy of this chart.*

Chapter 5 Checklist
How Do We Ensure That Data Drive Our Dialogues?

Goal	Long-Term Vision	First Steps
Data inform decisions that enhance the system of behavioral supports.	Staff collect and analyze data on behaviors, including questions related to *who*, *what*, *where*, and *when*.	☐ Tools such as the SRSS provide information about students potentially at risk and about areas of behavior that may require additional attention. ☐ Behavior documentation forms (BDFs) are adopted and faithfully used to gather data on behavior. ☐ Data are warehoused for future analysis using databases such as SWIS.
Data are used to specify behavioral needs and to monitor progress.	Staff recognizes that objective, observational data must be gathered to best support students at risk behaviorally.	☐ When students have not responded to Tier I behavioral supports, teams collaborate to gather and analyze observational data that inform students' behavioral challenges. ☐ Based on analyses of antecedents, data inform the nature of Tier 2 and 3 supports. ☐ Protocols are adopted to gather data to monitor the efficacy of behavioral supports and to measure student progress.

Goal	Long-Term Vision	First Steps
Data are regularly shared with the entire staff to celebrate and adjust efforts.	Staff regularly receives reports and analyses on behavioral trends, adjusting their allocation of resources, changing adult practices, and modifying school procedures based on collaborative analyses of the reports.	☐ Generate and analyze reports, at least monthly, to illustrate trends in behavior and celebrate successes and improvements. ☐ Collaboratively reflect upon data with a willingness to shift resources or to alter actions in an effort to improve behaviors. ☐ Collaborate to design initial support plans for students receiving the greatest number of BDFs.

*Visit **go.solution-tree.com/behavior** to download a copy of this chart.*

six

A Schoolwide Systems Approach

The previous chapters have covered a lot of ground and presented many challenges to those working in schools. Before describing how staff must systematically structure their schoolwide efforts, let's review what we have accomplished to this point:

- Staff members have committed to collaboratively supporting high expectations for student behavior and have articulated a focused set of common expectations.

- Staff members have constructed and communicated a matrix and have explicitly delivered targeted instruction to all students.

- Staff members have agreed to positively reinforce and recognize appropriate behaviors.

- Staff members have monitored and adjusted collaborative and creative ways of supporting and intervening with students in the yellow and red zones.

- Collaborative teams have met to support staff and students.

- Collaborative teams have engaged in data-driven dialogue regarding both individual students at risk for behavioral issues and behavioral areas requiring reinforcement.

How will we lead, manage, support, and sustain these efforts? This chapter connects the first six key components of a positive learning environment into a schoolwide systems approach.

In the absence of a consistent and effective action plan that ties together all of the components, our efforts will neither stand the test of time nor become an integrated part of the way we do things at our school. While a systematic approach is necessary, the model must also be flexible to allow for the strengths, needs, and styles of the adults in the school. Figure 6.1 (page 88) presents a plan for schools to develop, monitor, and implement a schoolwide approach that can result in positive outcomes (Coleman, 2006). While most school districts have some form of improvement cycle, we prefer this model set forth by the British Columbia Ministry of Education because it is centered on the concept of collaborative work.

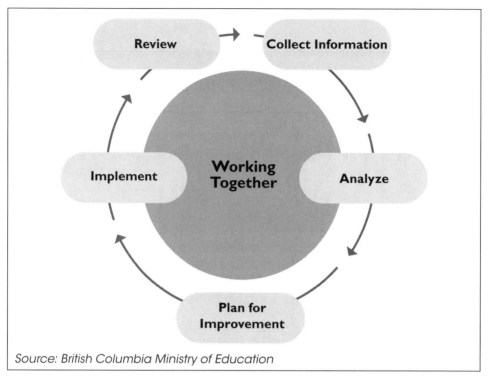

Source: British Columbia Ministry of Education

Figure 6.1: Collaborative inquiry model.

Some form of inquiry is foundational for effective organizations (Timperley, Wilson, Barrar, & Fung, 2007). It's a non-negotiable to our professional practice, a fundamental premise of PLCs—and it applies to everything we do in schools, including our efforts to improve students' successes in both academics and behavior. Next, we describe the cycle in relation to literacy, and later in this chapter, we relate it to behavior through an example.

Step 1: Collect Information

This step can be deceptively simple. Standardized assessments provide broad information but do not offer much insight into what specific challenges individual students might face. For more specific, detailed information, we may need more diagnostic assessments. It's the quality of information collected, not the quantity, that is important. Many schools suffer from what Robert Waterman (1987) identified as the DRIP (data rich but information poor) syndrome.

We'll use one school's academic goal—improving literacy skills across the curriculum—to illustrate this cycle. While the original focus of the work by this staff was academic, they were cognizant of the inextricable link with student behavior. At any school engaged in an inquiry cycle, staff members need to establish what measures, or indicators, they need to use and when they need to use them. In what specific areas of literacy will the school focus? Where are we starting? Which products will we examine to determine progress and to measure success? How many sources of information are required in order to present a clear picture? Will improving student success in literacy also improve student behavior and engagement?

Collecting helps us identify the information we want and to what end. It is the essential piece to engaging educators in the rich discourse about next steps and cannot occur in isolation from the other steps.

In this school example, between the fall of their seventh-grade year and the spring of their ninth-grade year, students were assessed in these four reading skills six times (twice per year). Team leaders kept track of this data from year to year and celebrated growth with the staff at the end of each school year. Teachers used the fall data to drive their instruction and planning and the spring data to celebrate the students' learning.

For example, the eighth-grade team of teachers (English, social studies, math, and science teachers) collected information by getting together for a few hours in the fall to assess the students' responses. As they collaborated, they made note of students' strengths and weaknesses. In addition to the specific notes they took for each student, they also collected gradewide data. After assessing all the tests, the team analyzed the data and determined the percentage of students who exceeded, fully met, minimally met, or did not meet grade-level expectations. Teachers used all of this information to plan for improvement and guide their planning and instruction for the duration of the year. Simultaneously, the principal and assistant principal monitored schoolwide behavior data for all students and tracked the individual behavior data for the students most at risk. Staff shared and compared this data. Not surprisingly, as literacy and engagement increased, behavior problems decreased.

Step 2: Analyze

The school goal of improving literacy across the curriculum was a starting point to examine the results for all students on a standardized test. Yet this examining of overall, aggregated scores determined by number of students reading at grade level provided little insight into individual student progress. Further analyses would involve examining scores on subskills or strands of literacy (note taking, reading pictures and graphs, presenting information in a variety of ways, and making inferences, for example) on a student-by-student and class-by-class basis over time. Teacher anecdotal evidence and office behavior data would reveal any connection between increased literacy success and decreased behavior problems.

We gain the most useful information from data when we approach our analyses with clear questions. Reading data reports like tea leaves, hoping that some nuggets of truth will emerge, is a risky and possibly misleading endeavor. Instead, this staff determined specific questions about standards and students and looked to the data to provide information about these areas. Data helped inform actions that needed to be taken to validate the efficacy of actions that have been taken. Schmoker (1999) suggests that "data make the invisible visible, revealing strengths and weaknesses that are easily concealed" (p. 44). Analysis of data can also help to break down teacher isolation, promote meaningful sharing, and indicate the impact of an instructional approach. In the case of this school, the staff came together across subjects and departments to analyze the literacy data and identify which of the subskills could fit within their separate curriculum areas. The more the teachers collaborated on the literacy data, the better able they were to identify both cross-curricular connections and student successes and failures.

Step 3: Plan for Improvement

Following analyses, in many cases, teachers may feel a little overwhelmed. What if the results show a bulk of students not meeting expectations? This is where the work may get messy, causing some teachers to avoid examining their practices and to step away from inconvenient truths. When analyses of data indicate action steps, we must be patient and determined. In this school example, the staff used the data and anecdotal evidence to implement new instructional strategies, interventions for students in need, and to differentiate instruction. Other possible responses emerge over time. In our literacy example, different PLC teams took ownership for developing improvement plans for literacy subskills, identifying ways in which their team could target instruction to help students meet goals that will be created with information from data analysis. Math and science teams, as well as elective area teachers in the shops and applied skills, took responsibility for interpreting pictures and graphs; social studies teachers addressed the comprehension of expository texts; and fine arts teachers focused on comparing and contrasting.

Evaluating common goals against a common focus helped in achieving a collective focus and also provided the opportunity for teachers to learn from each other in striving to achieve maximum results for students. This was true for the academic skills as well as the behavior management tasks. Teachers, collaborating more often on data based on common assessments, also had more conversations about challenging students. These conversations naturally included academic challenges and behavior challenges, as well as successes. Teachers learned from each other about what worked for their students. Fullan (2005) stresses the importance of working with the intent that "all levels of the system are expected to learn from their experiences" (p. 22). It is this deep learning that leads to improvements being sustainable over time.

Step 4: Implement

With your plans in place, do not assume that implementation will be easy. Only through a committed monitoring phase, taking action to produce early results for analysis, and intervening in situations with poor results (despite good intentions) will our efforts make a difference for students. In our literacy example, the teachers agreed upon team meeting norms in which sharing of strategies would occur during a portion of all team and staff meetings. Staff also agreed to try all agreed-upon strategies; team leaders were identified to lead the monitoring of progress on each goal. The role of the school leader is critical in this step. Leaders can further the implementation phase by catching teachers doing the right thing. Acknowledging the impact of a new instructional approach or measured risk taking by a teacher to address an emerging concern creates a sense of unity in a staff and fosters a team approach. Leaders also assist the implementation step by providing focus. This must be evident through actions to avoid becoming what Reeves (2004) identifies as leaders who espouse the "virtues of focus even as they develop strategic plans that are more closely linked to deforestation than to improved student achievement" (p. 59). In this school's literacy example, the principal supported the team leaders in learning how to lead these collaborative, student-focused meetings. This included helping team leaders and the whole staff recognize the connection between increased academic success and decreased behavior issues.

Step 5: Review

In the review phase, all of your hard efforts are put to the test when you ask the key question, "Did it work?" The review step speaks to the need to critically analyze strategies utilized against results achieved. To complete our look at the school-based literacy example, this step involved data analysis at the classroom and individual student levels across subject areas and against the subskills. It involved collaboration sessions to review the success of individual strategies, and observations during which teachers viewed colleagues using the identified strategies. Teachers observing each other naturally commented on classroom management and behavior at the same time as discussing successful instruction and assessment strategies.

Collecting and analyzing data shows schools how they are progressing toward improving their outcomes and achievements. Schmoker (1999) stated, "Common goals that are regularly evaluated against common measures—data—sustain collective focus and reveal the best opportunities for practitioners to learn from each other and hence to get better results" (p. 45). This step ties together intention and results to propel educators forward as they work with students to close the achievement gap. In the literacy example, the staff did just that.

The following example illustrates the five-step process.

Cliff Street Elementary had a long-term literacy goal to improve student scores on the reading component of the mandated standardized test. The staff initially had difficulty getting excited about this district-mandated goal. However, the goal started coming alive during monthly staff meetings when the principal and teachers started sharing short-term success stories of individual kids in their classes. Under the agenda item "Kids First," the principal would prime the pump with observations of great individual student progress and promising practices in the classrooms. The focus was twofold: academic success and improved behavior. Soon other staff felt comfortable sharing more individual short-term successes. People began to see the difference they were making and were congratulating one another. Collaborative conversations about student progress, successful strategies, and school climate increased. Soon, all staff eagerly analyzed academic and behavior data every term, noting progress and trends, and reflecting on their efforts as individuals and grade-level groups. "Great News" bulletins were sent home to parents. The principal praised individuals and the staff as a whole. He bragged about them often. In just over one year, staff and students met and exceeded the literacy goal target while at the same time substantially decreasing office referrals. The principal celebrated with a giant decorated cake and lots of community publicity. The successes started small, with individual student progress, and grew to include cross-grade comparisons and celebrations until the long-term schoolwide goal was met. Informal and formal celebrations and recognition happened throughout the journey.

Our goal should be to become informed by data. To be informed by data as an individual teacher can improve a classroom. To be informed by data as a collaborative team will transform a school.

Working Together

Perhaps the single most precious resource in education today is time. Time to communicate as colleagues ranks as the biggest concern we have heard in our work with educators across North America. In the absence of this time, educators develop a bunker mentality that leads them to focus on their own classroom environment while losing touch with the greater school community. It results in the pockets of brilliance that emanate in every school, but it dissuades any collective momentum being established that really propels a school forward. We can't emphasize enough the notion that "none of us is as smart as all of us" and that the key to sustainable, long-term growth in schools hinges on the collective response to challenges that inevitably exist. As Roland Barth (2006) notes:

> The nature of relationships among the adults within a school has a greater influence upon the character and quality of a school and on student accomplishment than anything else. (p. 8)

Barth suggests that relationships between and among administrators and teachers invariably dictate relationships between teachers and their students and between educators and parents. Relationships among educators define all relationships within a school's culture. Thus, finding the time to do our essential work collaboratively becomes non-negotiable. Barth (2006) concluded:

> Empowerment, recognition, satisfaction, and success in our work—all in scarce supply within our schools—will never stem from going it alone as a masterful teacher, principal, or student, no matter how accomplished one is. Empowerment, recognition, satisfaction and success come only from being an active participant within a masterful group—a group of colleagues. (p. 13)

Positive relationships are a key to successfully implementing a schoolwide approach to successful behavioral supports. Saphier and King (1985) identified characteristics that support a healthy school culture and the development of positive relationships:

- Collegiality
- High expectations
- Trust and confidence
- Tangible support
- Appreciation and recognition
- Involvement in decision making

These characteristics are essential to PLCs and to a schoolwide systems approach to positive learning environments. While the time to communicate is essential, it must be coupled with building staff capacity. Michael Fullan (2005) describes this as the development of "collective ability—dispositions, skills, knowledge, motivation, and resources—to act together to bring about positive change" (p. 4). This happens as a result of creating opportunities for teachers to work together.

Putting It All Together

In this book, we have set out to combine the best elements of PLCs, PBIS, and features of RTI to help you improve student behavior. This may seem like a tall order in an era of significant changes in schools that may lead staffs to try many different strategies while perfecting none. Douglas Reeves (2010) talks about the "Law of Initiative Fatigue," which states:

> When the number of initiatives increases while time, resources, and emotional energy are constant, then each new initiative—no matter how well conceived or well intentioned—will receive fewer minutes, dollars, and ounces of emotional energy than its predecessors. (p. 27)

The solution to overcoming the law lies, in part, in establishing a clear focus in planning for success and integrating new initiatives with the current way of conducting education. In this environment, schools can take on the initiatives we have described in this book and thrive.

Since its opening four years ago, one elementary school in which we've worked has made establishing a system of behavioral supports a primary area of focus for the school. This is that school's story.

A Focus on Behavioral Support

Students at Palmer Elementary come from diverse ethnic backgrounds, with a balance between African American (33 percent), Hispanic (33 percent), and Caucasian (33 percent) students. Students face harsh realities on a daily basis, including challenging socioeconomic conditions. Nearly every student lives in a high-density apartment dwelling, and the mobility rate is an extraordinarily high 55 percent.

More than 75 percent of students qualified for free or reduced-price lunch. The students received bilingual education on the campus, where thirty-five separate languages were spoken. The campus also housed the district self-contained classes for students diagnosed with severe behavioral disorders. Reteaching schoolwide rules and expectations is a constant reality at this school, where both student and staff turnover is high. The most prominent concern at this school was physical aggression.

The school first collected and analyzed information, as shown in figure 6.2. This graph shows the number of referrals for aggression for the first and second quarters of the 2007–2008 and 2008–2009 school years. Although the first quarter numbers in the 2008–2009 school year were higher than the previous year (2007–2008), as shown in tables 6.1 and 6.2 (pages 95–96), they noted dramatic improvements during the second quarter, neither coincidentally nor surprisingly. This was the time period in which a system of behavioral supports was first implemented.

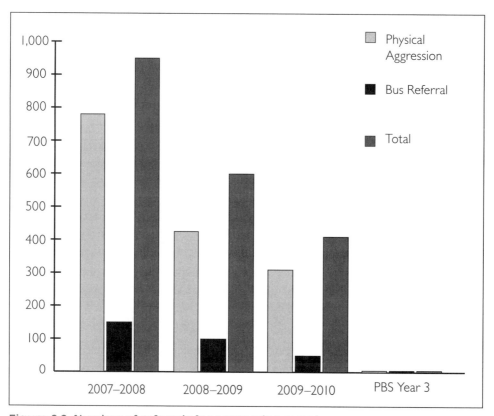

Figure 6.2: Number of referrals for aggression over two years.

Table 6.1: Referral Comparison Before Behavioral Supports

Referrals for First Nine Weeks (2007–2008)		Referrals for Second Nine Weeks (2007–2008)	
Physical aggression	19	Bus misconduct	36
Bus misconduct	18	Conflict with another student	8
Damaged school property	1	Damaged school property	4
Mischief/horseplay	3	Disturbing class	24
Disrupting school environment	2	Fighting	2
Conflict w/another student	8	Insubordination	12
Disturbing class or students	20	Mischief/horseplay	9
Fighting	2	Misconduct	3
Misconduct	1	Physical aggression	33
Profane or obscene language	1	Profanity	7
Truancy	1	Theft	1
Verbal/written/graphic abuse	1	Verbal/written/graphic abuse	1
Total	77	Total	140

Table 6.2: Referral Comparison for Second Nine Weeks After Implementing Behavior Supports

Referrals for First Nine Weeks (2008–2009)		Referrals for Second Nine Weeks (2008–2009)	
Physical aggression	53	Bus misconduct	1
Bus misconduct	43	Conflict with another student	0
Damaged school property	5	Damaged school property	1
Mischief/horseplay	2	Disturbing class	1
Disrupting school environment	2	Fighting	0
Obscene gesture	1	Insubordination	0
Persistent misbehavior	4	Mischief/horseplay	0
False alarm	1	Misconduct	0

continued →

Referrals for First Nine Weeks (2008–2009)		Referrals for Second Nine Weeks (2008–2009)	
Possession of illegal knife	1	Physical aggression	19
Threat of bodily injury	1	Profanity	4
Elopement from class	3	Theft	0
Theft	3	Verbal/written/graphic abuse	2
Elopement from campus	1	Elopement from class	1
Total	120	Total	29

A successful cycle at another elementary school in which we worked drove improvements in student behavior, led to a more focused academic climate, and contributed to large gains in student learning.

A Successful Cycle

Chris was the new principal of a school on the verge of entering program improvement status as a result of failing to meet adequate yearly progress. There was a sense that something needed to be done at the school, but there was no new money or personnel. Staff reported that there were often dozens of students sitting in the front office waiting to be seen by the principal—teachers felt as though they lacked the tools and skills to successfully manage behaviors in the classrooms. There was no longer an assistant principal at the school because of budget cuts, so dealing with the number of students sent to the office was an even greater challenge. Staff also spoke of lackadaisical students and unstructured recesses and lunch times where students wandered aimlessly, played games with no discernable rules, and often got into physical conflicts.

A system of behavioral supports seemed a logical initiative to consider, and staff agreed that student misbehavior was a huge concern. The challenge was convincing staff that students could behave better and defining what types of behavior were desired. Like many schools, the staff agreed that expecting students to be respectful, responsible, and ready to learn was a sensible set of broad expectations.

After listening to staff complain about students well known for their constant misbehavior, Chris asked staff to tell stories of students who worked hard and who had made significant behavioral and/or academic growth.

Then the group looked at data. The data told a story that contrasted with perceptions. In a school in which 75 percent of students were Latino and 25 percent were Caucasian, 14 of the 20 students receiving the highest number of office referrals the previous year were Caucasian. The staff had accepted the stereotype that Latino students would misbehave more than white students. The data encouraged staff to challenge their own stereotypes and helped them open their minds for the work ahead.

The staff adopted the common expectations of respect, responsibility, and readiness, and then began the job of crafting a matrix. They collected and reviewed the matrices and behavior documentation forms (BDFs) of neighboring schools that had successfully implemented and sustained systems of behavioral supports. The school already had positive reinforcements—Caught Being Good cards, nicknamed "blue cards." All staff agreed to use blue cards to recognize students whose behaviors met expectations as defined by the matrix.

They planned during the second half of their first year together, and then staff set aside a half day at the beginning of the following school year to explicitly teach students behavioral expectations in each setting, as communicated within the matrix. Half of the staff created minilessons, and the other half supervised students during their tour of each behavioral station. All teachers reinforced expectations within their classrooms throughout the rest of the day, week, and month.

The staff considered various ways of acknowledging students for their positive behaviors and agreed to recognize each student who accumulated twenty-five blue cards with a certificate, signed by the principal, which they could use as a coupon for a free book from the office library. Through donations from private and corporate sources, the school had an impressive collection of used and new books. Of course, students also took the certificates home to share with their parents.

In fact, communicating high expectations to parents was a key and constant feature of the work. Staff visited parent-teacher organization meetings; the matrix was posted on the school's marquee and website and explained to the town's city council (along with a request for funds to support the work); and teachers reinforced the system of supports during back-to-school night and during parent conferences.

The BDF and the School-Wide Information System (SWIS) were key. Chris took the responsibility of entering data from every BDF into SWIS every day, a modest task of only ten to fifteen minutes. This allowed him to get a quick look at the types of students and infractions that were occurring in a timely manner. He learned that pulling students from their classroom to the office to be chastised for their misdeeds often further satisfied their reason for the misbehavior in the first place—they avoided class time. So Chris asked teachers if he could visit classes and quickly address infractions during a thirty- to sixty-second conversation right outside the classroom door. This practice served many purposes: teachers knew he was following through on infractions firmly and quickly. Students who made bad decisions received immediate feedback in a respectful way, with a review of expectations and an encouraging word for the future. Other students in classrooms were reminded that high expectations reflected the way in which business was done at their school.

Chris visited classrooms for this reason every day, but came bearing more than BDFs. He also brought any certificates earned by students for accumulating twenty-five blue cards. While a review of BDFs with students was a private affair, he asked teachers if he could publicly acknowledge a student in the front of the classroom who earned a certificate—if the one or two minutes needed would not detract from instruction. This also provided an opportunity for the teacher and Chris to remind students of expectations and the rewards of hard work.

The school was lucky enough to have one hour per week when teacher teams could meet during their instructional day. Staff agreed to take a portion of this time to discuss students who were at risk, including those experiencing difficulty with behaviors. Teachers shared these names with Chris, and they collaboratively discussed behavior at every staff meeting. They agreed upon a standard behavior contract for students experiencing difficulties in class (a Tier 1 support) and brainstormed responses to more complex misbehavior, including those occurring during recess and lunch.

Analyses of SWIS data indicated that physical contact was a concern for all grades, particularly during morning recess. The staff agreed to shift some supervision coverage from the later recess to the earlier recess, and Chris used upcoming recesses to review expectations with all students in the gymnasium. Other students required more intensive supports. The staff individualized solutions for these students, given the unique nature of their difficulties.

The staff was blown away by the results. Student behavior changed—physical contact ceased to be the biggest concern. The biggest concern later became following directions within the classroom, a need the team approached with same collaborative spirit, albeit with a new sense of confidence. When state test results were released, the staff was again blown away: the percentage of students meeting or exceeding state standards in both reading and mathematics more than doubled.

The staff experienced frustrations, of course, such as when students forgot the rules over winter break. Chris quickly retaught expectations over a series of recesses and lunch periods, and teachers reinforced them during class time. And they constantly found themselves creatively refining supports for red-zone students. What worked one week for students in the red zone did not necessarily work the next week, but several of these students passed the state tests, an achievement that probably would not have been realized without the system of behavioral supports.

After four years, student achievement for all students was at an all-time high, the school had avoided the program improvement classification, and the school was receiving recognition for the hard work and successes of students and staff.

A Systematic Approach

Educators may think that these results can't be replicated in their schools. They may think there was something special about the schools in these examples and those throughout the book. Perhaps there was something special—a commitment to working collaboratively, holding high expectations for students and adults, and exhibiting the power of persistence.

Whether we are implementing academic or behavioral interventions, at least one attribute is non-negotiable: our efforts must be systematic. There are schools across North America with pockets of excellence—teachers or teams that provide exceptional support to students—where students perform at the very highest levels. Our goal is loftier: we expect high levels of achievement, both academic and behavioral, for all. To achieve this, the entire school must commit to all seven keys to a positive learning environment.

Chapter 6 Checklist
How Do We Lead a Schoolwide Systems Approach?

Goal	Long-Term Vision	First Steps
Make a cycle of inquiry the way business is done at the school.	Staff continuously improves, using a cycle of inquiry to collaboratively analyze, execute, and reflect.	☐ Analyze data on student performance in both the behavioral and academic domains to identify strengths and areas for growth. ☐ Collaboratively develop and cooperatively implement an action plan designed to meet specifically identified needs. ☐ Carefully monitor and adjust improvement efforts to ensure they are successful.
School leaders follow up, celebrate, and redirect.	Staff embraces the responsibility and the power of immediate feedback for students and staff regarding behavioral areas of concern.	☐ Process BDFs on a daily basis, providing immediate reinforcement to the student and the school. ☐ Agree upon and regularly utilize positive reinforcers to recognize consistently positive behaviors and to start to reteach and reinforce the behaviors of students requiring intervention.

Goal	Long-Term Vision	First Steps
School leaders follow up, celebrate, and redirect. *(continued)*		☐ Communicate with all staff, ensuring that the school's efforts in sustaining a positive learning environment are consistent.
Intensively focus improvement efforts.	Staff understands and embraces a focused set of initiatives, understanding that success will result in broad improvements.	☐ Narrow areas of focus are based on data and needs. ☐ Collaborative teams devote their work to helping students and staff reach the high expectations that are defined by these areas of focus. ☐ Human and material resources are dedicated to these areas of focus. ☐ Reflect upon and make adjustments to ensure that success is guaranteed.

*Visit **go.solution-tree.com/behavior** to download a copy of this chart.*

epilogue

Throughout our careers, we have had many opportunities to see the world of education from a variety of perspectives. Whatever school we visit—be it urban or rural, large or small, wealthy or poor—we encounter educators facing similar challenges. Fortunately, we also find educators committed to making positive change despite these challenges. Their stories are the stories in this book.

We are indebted to the hundreds of educators who have shared their stories with us and who have so clearly made a difference in the lives of their students. If we believe that every student is a success story waiting to be told, our role as educators is to empower them and help them articulate their stories. As we've shown with some of the stories in this book, it is rarely a specific subject or content that makes the difference to a child. Rather, it is the relationship with caring adults who model appropriate behavior that ensures that the story has a happy ending. We've encountered many educators in our work who are givers of hope. It is this hope that allows us to move forward and to overcome challenges.

Educators and parents all want their kids to be the success stories that are told. We are convinced by the evidence, the data, and our experiences that the seven keys outlined in this book really do create the positive learning environment that we all know is best for kids.

Ainsworth, L. (2003). *Power standards: Identifying the standards that matter the most.* Englewood, CO: Lead and Learn Press.

Barth, R. (2006). Improving professional practice. *Educational Leadership, 63*(6), 8–13.

Bennett, B., & Rolheiser, C. (2001). *Beyond Monet: The artful science of instructional integration.* Toronto, ON: Bookation.

Biglan, A. (1995). *Changing cultural practices: A contextualistic framework for intervention research.* Reno, NV: Context Press.

Bolman, L., & Deal, T. (2002). *Reframing the path to school leadership: A guide for teachers and principals.* Thousand Oaks, CA: Corwin Press.

Boyer, E. (1995). *The basic school: A community for learning.* San Francisco: Jossey-Bass.

Buffum, A., Mattos, M., & Weber, C. (2009). *Pyramid response to intervention: RTI, professional learning communities, and how to respond when kids don't learn.* Bloomington, IN: Solution Tree Press.

Cameron, J., & Pierce, W. D. (2006). *Rewards and intrinsic motivation: Resolving the controversy.* Charlotte, NC: Information Age.

Coleman, C. (2003). Beyond tokens and rewards. *Adminfo, 16*(2), 7–8.

Coleman, C. (2006, February 22). *Innovation & improvement—school planning councils* [webcast]. Accessed at http://www.insinc.com/ministryofeducation/20060222/ on June 1, 2011. Vancouver: British Columbia Ministry of Education.

Collins, J. (2001). Good to great: Why some companies make the leap . . . and others don't. New York: HarperCollins.

Collins, J., & Porras, J. (1997). *Built to last: Successful habits of visionary companies.* New York: Harper Business.

Coloroso, B. (2001). *Kids are worth it.* Toronto, ON: Penguin Books.

Colvin, G., & Sugai, G. (1988). Proactive strategies for managing social behavior problems: An instructional approach. *Education and Treatment of Children, 11,* 341–348.

Covey, S. (1989). *The 7 habits of highly effective people: Powerful lessons in personal change.* New York: Fireside.

Cregor, M. (2008). The building blocks of positive behavior. *Teaching Tolerance.* Accessed at www.tolerance.org/magazine/number-34-fall-2008/building-blocks-positive-behavior on June 1, 2011.

Curwin, R. L., Mendler, A. N., & Mendler, B. D. (2008). *Discipline with dignity: New challenges, new solutions.* Alexandria, VA: Association for Supervision and Curriculum Development.

Davies, A. (2007). Involving students in the classroom assessment process. In D. Reeves (Ed.), *Ahead of the curve: The power of assessment to transform teaching and learning* (pp. 31–57). Bloomington, IN: Solution Tree Press.

Dishion, T. J., & Patterson, G. R. (1997). The timing and severity of antisocial behavior: Three hypotheses within an ecological framework. In D. Stoff, J. Brieling, & J. Maser (Eds.), *Handbook of antisocial behavior* (pp. 205–217). New York: Wiley.

Drummond, T. (1993). *The student risk screening scale (SRSS).* Grants Pass, OR: Josephine County Mental Health Program.

DuFour, R., DuFour, R., & Eaker, R. (2008). *Revisiting professional learning communities at work: New insights for improving schools.* Bloomington, IN: Solution Tree Press.

DuFour, R., DuFour, R., Eaker, R., & Karhanek, G. (2004). *Whatever it takes: How professional learning communities respond when kids don't learn.* Bloomington, IN: Solution Tree Press.

DuFour, R., DuFour, R., Eaker, R., & Many, T. (2006). *Learning by doing: A handbook for professional learning communities at work.* Bloomington, IN: Solution Tree Press.

DuFour, R., DuFour, R., Eaker, R., & Many, T. (2010). *Learning by doing: A handbook for professional learning communities at work* (2nd ed.). Bloomington, IN: Solution Tree Press.

DuFour, R., Eaker, R., & DuFour, R. (Eds.). (2005). *On common ground: The power of professional learning communities.* Bloomington, IN: Solution Tree Press.

Ernsperger, L. (2002). *Keys to success for teaching students with autism.* Arlington, TX: Future Horizons.

Fullan, M. (2003). *The moral imperative of school leadership.* Thousand Oaks, CA: Corwin Press.

Fullan, M. (2005). *Leadership and sustainability: System thinkers in action.* Thousand Oaks, CA: Corwin Press.

Fullan, M., Crevola, C., Hill, P. (2006). *Breakthrough.* Thousand Oaks, CA: Corwin Press.

Ginott, H. (1976). *Teacher and child.* New York: Avon.

Gladwell, M. (2009). *What the dog saw: And other adventures.* New York: Little, Brown.

Glasser, W. (1998). *Choice theory.* New York: HarperCollins.

Glaze, A., & Mattingly, R. (2008). *Class interrupted: Strategies for positive behaviour (school-wide focus).* Edmonton, AB: Pearson.

Good, T. L. (2010). Forty years of research on teaching 1968–2008: What do we know now that we didn't know then? In R. J. Marzano (Ed.), *On excellence in teaching* (pp. 31–62). Bloomington, IN: Solution Tree Press.

Gossen, D. C. (1998). *Restitution: Restructuring school discipline* (facilitator's guide). Chapel Hill, NC: New View.

Harwayne, S. (1999). *Going public: Priorities and practice at the Manhattan new school.* Portsmouth, NH: Heineman.

Hawkins, J. D., Catalano, R. F., Kosterman, R., Abbott, R., & Hill, K. G. (1999). Preventing adolescent health-risk behaviors by strengthening protection during childhood. *Archives of Pediatrics & Adolescent Medicine, 153*, 226–234.

Hawkins, J. D., Harlow, C., O'Connor, P., & Campbell, A. (1994). *Literacy behind prison walls.* Washington, DC: National Center for Education Statistics.

Hierck, T. (2009a). Differentiated pathways to success. In T. Guskey (Ed.), *The teacher as assessment leader* (pp. 249–262). Bloomington, IN: Solution Tree Press.

Hierck, T. (2009b). Formative assessment, transformative relationships. In T. Guskey (Ed.), *The principal as assessment leader* (pp. 245–264). Bloomington, IN: Solution Tree Press.

Horner, R. H., Sugai, G., & Todd, A. W. (2001). "Data" need not be a four-letter word: Using data to improve school-wide discipline. *Beyond Behaviour, 2*(1), 20–22.

Hulley, W., & Dier, L. (2008). *Getting by or getting better.* Bloomington, IN: Solution Tree Press.

Individuals with Disabilities Education Improvement Act, 20 U.S.C. § 1400 (2004).

Jackson, R. (2009). *Never work harder than your students.* Alexandria, VA: Association for Supervision and Curriculum Development.

Kohn, A. (1996). *Beyond discipline: From compliance to community.* Alexandria, VA: Association for Supervision and Curriculum Development.

Kohn, A. (2005). Unconditional teaching. *Educational Leadership, 63*(1), 20–25.

Kouzes, J., & Posner, B. (1987). *The leadership challenge: How to get extraordinary things done in organizations.* San Francisco: Jossey-Bass.

Lane, K. L., Kalberg, J. R., Lambert, E. W., Crnobori, M., & Bruhn, A. L. (2009). A comparison of systematic screening tools for emotional and behavioral disorders. *Journal of Emotional and Behavioral Disorders, 17*(2), 93–105.

Lane, T. W., & Murakami, J. (1987). School programs for delinquency prevention and intervention. In E. K. Morris & C. J. Braukmann (Eds.), *Behavioral approaches to crime and delinquency: A handbook of application, research, and concepts* (pp. 305–327). New York: Plenum Press.

Lewis, T. J., & Sugai, G. (1999). Effective behaviour support: A systems approach to proactive school-wide management. *Focus on Exceptional Children, 31*(6), 1–24.

Lezotte, L. (1997). *Learning for all.* Okemos, MI: Effective Schools Products.

Marzano, R. J. (2003). *What works in schools: Translating research into action.* Alexandria, VA: Association for Supervision and Curriculum Development.

Marzano, R. J. (2007). *The art and science of teaching: A comprehensive framework for effective instruction.* Alexandria, VA: Association for Supervision and Curriculum Development.

Marzano, R. J. (2010). Developing expert teachers. In R. J. Marzano (Ed.), *On excellence in teaching* (pp. 213–245). Bloomington, IN: Solution Tree Press.

Marzano, R. J., & Haystead, M. (2008). *Making standards useful in the classroom.* Alexandria, VA: Association for Supervision and Curriculum Development.

Marzano, R. J., Marzano, J. S., & Pickering, D. J. (2003). *Classroom management that works: Research based strategies for every teacher.* Alexandria, VA: Association for Supervision and Curriculum Development.

Maslow, A. (1954). *Motivation and personality.* New York: Harper.

McCreary Centre Society. (2003). *Healthy youth development: Highlights from the 2003 adolescent health survey III.* Vancouver, BC: Author.

Mendler, A. N., & Curwin, R. L. (1999). *Discipline with dignity for challenging youth.* Bloomington, IN: Solution Tree Press.

Muhammad, A. (2009). *Transforming school culture: How to overcome staff division.* Bloomington, IN: Solution Tree Press.

O'Neill, J., & Conzemius, A. (2006). *The power of SMART goals: Using goals to improve student learning.* Bloomington, IN: Solution Tree Press.

OSEP Technical Assistance Center on Positive Behavioral Interventions & Support. (2011). *School-wide PBIS.* Accessed at http://www.pbis.org/school/default.aspx on June 2, 2011.

Patterson, K., Grenny, J., Maxfield, D., McMillan, R., & Switzler, A. (2008). *Influencer: The power to change anything.* New York: McGraw-Hill.

Reeves, D. (2004). *Accountability for learning: How teachers and school leaders can take charge.* Alexandria, VA: Association for Supervision and Curriculum Development.

Reeves, D. (2010). *Transforming professional development into student results.* Alexandria, VA: Association for Supervision and Curriculum Development.

Reithaug, D. (1998). *Orchestrating positive and practical behaviour plans.* West Vancouver, BC: Stirling Head.

Rogers, C. R. (1961). *On becoming a person: A therapist's view of psychotherapy.* New York: Mariner Books.

Saphier, J., & King, M. (1985). Good seeds grow in strong cultures. *Educational Leadership, 42*(6), 67–74.

Schmoker, M. (1999). *Results: The key to continuous school improvement.* Alexandria, VA: Association for Supervision and Curriculum Development.

Senge, P. (1990). *The fifth discipline: The art and practice of the learning organization.* New York: Currency Doubleday.

Sergiovanni, T. (1992). *Moral leadership: Getting to the heart of school improvement.* San Francisco: Jossey-Bass.

Skinner, B. F. (1948). *Walden two.* New York: Macmillan.

Stiggins, R. (2007). Assessment for learning: An essential foundation of productive instruction. In D. Reeves (Ed.), *Ahead of the curve: The power of assessment to transform teaching and learning* (pp. 59–76). Bloomington, IN: Solution Tree Press.

Sugai, G., & Colvin, G. (2004). *Positive behaviour support: Non-classroom management: Self-assessment.* Accessed at www.pbis.ocde.us/Assets/PBIS/downloads/Non+Classroom+Self+Assessment.pdf on May 24, 2011.

Sugai, G., & Horner, R. R. (2006). A promising approach for expanding and sustaining schoolwide positive behavior support. *School Psychology Review*, *35*(2), 245–259.

Sugai, G., & Horner, R. R. (2011). Behavior function: Staying close to what we know. *PBIS Newsletter*, *1*(1). Accessed at www.pbis.org/pbis_newsletter/volume_1/issue1.aspx on April 26, 2011.

Sulzer-Azaroff, B., & Mayer, R. (1991). *Behavior analysis for lasting change*. Fort Worth, TX: Holt, Reinhart & Winston.

Timperley, H., Wilson, A., Barrar, H., & Fung, I. (2007). *Teacher professional learning and development: Best evidence synthesis iteration*. Wellington, New Zealand: Ministry of Education.

U.S. Department of Education Office of Special Education and Rehabilitative Services. (2002). *A new era: Revitalizing special education for children and their families*. Washington, DC: Author.

Walker, H. M., Colvin, G., & Ramsey, E. (1995). *Antisocial behavior in school: Strategies and best practices*. Pacific Grove, CA: Brooks/Cole.

Waterman, R. (1987). *The renewal factor: How the best get and keep the competitive edge*. New York: Bantam Books.

creating acceptable alternatives, 65–66
description of, 20
expectations and providing positive,
    28–29
positive, 56–57
problems, handling, 68–69
Switzler, A., 23

T
targeted instruction. *See* instruction,
  targeted
teachers
    impact of, 3–5
    role of, 39

Todd, A. W., 6
trust, collaborative teams and, 73–74

U
universal screening, 75–78

W
Walker, H. M., 16
wannabes, 15
Waterman, R., 88
Weber, C., 11
What Works in Schools (Marzano), 45

Y
yellow zone, 14, 15

Pyramid Response to Intervention
RTI, Professional Learning Communities, and How to Respond When Kids Don't Learn
By Austin Buffum, Mike Mattos, and Chris Weber
Accessible language and compelling stories illustrate how RTI is most effective when built on the Professional Learning Communities at Work™ process. Written by award-winning educators, this book details three tiers of interventions—from basic to intensive—and includes implementation ideas.
BKF251

Understanding Response to Intervention
A Practical Guide to Systemic Implementation
By Robert Howell, Sandra Patton, and Margaret Deiotte
Whether you want a basic understanding of RTI or desire thorough knowledge for district-level implementation, you need this book. Understand the nuts and bolts of RTI. Follow clear examples of effective practices that include systems and checklists to assess your RTI progress.
BKF253

Behave Yourself!
Helping Students Plan to Do Better
By Ambrose Panico
Learn specific strategies for developing behavior intervention plans (BIPs) that lead to long-term, positive change for general and special education students. The author outlines a practical five-step Plan to Do Better approach and provides reproducibles that ease the information-gathering process.
BKF267

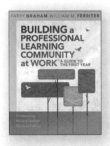

Building a Professional Learning Community at Work™
A Guide to the First Year
By Parry Graham and William M. Ferriter
This play-by-play guide to implementing PLC concepts uses a story to focus each chapter. The authors analyze the story, highlighting good decisions and mistakes. They offer research behind best practice and wrap up each chapter with practical recommendations and tools.
BKF319

Visit solution-tree.com or call 800.733.6786 to order.

Solution Tree | Press
a division of

Solution Tree

Wait! Your professional development journey doesn't have to end with the last pages of this book.

We realize improving student learning doesn't happen overnight. And your school or district shouldn't be left to puzzle out all the details of this process alone.

No matter where you are on the journey, we're committed to helping you get to the next stage.

Take advantage of everything from **custom workshops** to **keynote presentations** and **interactive web and video conferencing**. We can even help you develop an action plan tailored to fit your specific needs.

Let's get the conversation started.

Call 888.763.9045 today.